50 Ways YOU Can Show George the Door in 2004

Ben Cohen and Jason Salzman

Westview
PRESS

A Member of the Perseus Books Group

Copyright © 2004 by Westview Press, a Member of the Perseus Books Group.

Ben Cohen authored this book on behalf of himself and not on behalf of Ben & Jerry's, which is not associated with this book.

Published in the United States of America by Westview Press, A Member of the Perseus Books Group, 5500 Central Avenue, Boulder, Colorado 80301–2877, and in the United Kingdom by Westview Press, 12 Hid's Copse Road, Cumnor Hill, Oxford OX2 9JJ.

Find us on the world wide web at www.westviewpress.com.

Westview Press books are available at special discounts for bulk purchases in the United States by corporations, institutions, and other organizations. For more information, please contact the Special Markets Department at the Perseus Books Group, 11 Cambridge Center, Cambridge, MA 02142, or call (617) 252–5298, (800) 255-1514 or email special.markets@perseus-books.com.

A Cataloging-in-Publication data record for this book is available from the Library of Congress.
ISBN 0–8133–4282-1

The paper used in this publication meets the requirements of the American National Standard for Permanence of Paper for Printed Library Materials Z39.48–1984.

10 9 8 7 6 5 4 3

Dedication

We dedicate this book to defeating George W. Bush in November—and to Pete Seeger, who inspired a generation.

CONTENTS

Acknowledgments

Our top acknowledgments go to Jason's wife, Anne Button, who directed her expert editing, writing, and research skills toward improving every aspect of the manuscript, and to Aretha Cohen, Ben's daughter, who helped keep it all in perspective.

All the people at Westview Press, especially our editor Steve Catalano, were a pleasure to work with and incredibly supportive of the project. Gary Ferdman's encouragement and input also helped get this book off the ground.

These kind folks commented on drafts of the manuscript, in whole or in part: Heather Booth, Dan Carol, Jenny Davies-Schley, Jill Hanauer, Jaci Kelleher, Duane Peterson, and Aaron Toso. Kendra Beckwith provided life-saving research assistance.

Thanks to Natalie Blais, Jane and Jerry Button, Charlie Davies-Schley, Andrew Greenblatt, Jerry Greenfield, David Grinspoon, Amy Sheber-Howard, Emily Katzenstein, Mike Lund, Lois Lurie, Lauren Martens, Heller McDermott, Joanne and Manny Salzman and family, Tory Read, Dave Reed, Jack Shanahan, Darcy Scott-Martin, Maya Sunshine, Meghan Toso, Waggles, and Leo Wiegman.

Jason acknowledges his seven-year-old son, Dylan, who never stops, and his three-year-old daughter, Nell, who never sleeps.

We're grateful to Jesse Mangerson for his illustrations and to John Boak for designing the "Another Business for Voter Registration" sign.

★ INTRODUCTION: WALK YOUR TALK ★

We've talked, talked, talked, and talked for four years about how much of a disaster George W. Bush has been—for the economy, the environment, schools, international relations, civil liberties, and most everything else we care about at home and abroad.

Now it's time to do everything we can to vote him out in November.

That's why we wrote this book—so all of us who are so worked up about Bush can do something productive to remove him from office.

And that means all of us—whether you have just a few minutes to spare, a few days, or months of free time on your hands. Whether you are a practical, everyday citizen or a frothing anti-Bush activist, we've got a full menu of options, allowing you to utilize whatever talent and inspiration you've got.

This book has everything you need to help defeat Bush—how you can help register voters, win in swing states, and mobilize supporters on Election Day. Do you own a pet? We have ideas for dressing Waggles in Vote-Bush-Out garb. Like to sing? We've got Bush parody songs. Ditto poetry. Enjoy drama? We have costume suggestions. If you're a talker, walker, joker, businessperson, Internet addict, or media hound, there are all kinds of choices for you to take action to help remove the current administration from the White House.

Politics Is Fun?

A lot of politics is tedious, but too many people think that all of it is boring. It isn't. In fact, the most effective political action is as entertaining for the participants as it is for the spectators. That's why our

fifty suggestions for helping defeat Bush include ideas to make a difference and have fun at the same time. And while there are plenty of
things you can do on your own, you'll have more fun—and have a
greater impact—if you find a few people to take action with you.

How the Book Is Organized

Under each of our fifty suggested actions, we describe different ideas
for three distinct types of citizens:

 actions for practical, concerned, and busy people.

These folks want Bush to go, but—between working, doing laundry,
paying bills, and squeezing in quality time with their kids or friends—
they don't have a lot of free time. So we offer ways to help that don't
require much time but are nonetheless strategic and effective.

 actions for anti-Bush patriots with time to spare.

These are people so incensed at Bush that they're ready to carve out
an hour here or there from their busy lives to dedicate to regime
change at home. Or maybe they've got serious time on their hands
because they've lost their jobs thanks to Bush. Maybe they're retired.
Maybe they're students on summer break. Whoever they are, we've
got action ideas for them that require anywhere from a few hours to
a few weeks or more.

 actions for anybody-but-Bush guerillas.

Guerillas, as we affectionately call them, are the types of people who
are impatient with any action tinged with passivity—or, worse, insti-
tutionosis, which they see as an ailment of big organizations that move
too slowly. Guerillas are idealistic and artistic. They love political
street theater. They will work late at night to meet deadlines, and they
will adjust their schedules to make time for doing what needs to be
done to re-defeat Bush. We've devised a set of actions for guerillas
that are edgy, and we advise all guerillas to respect local customs and
mores and not do anything illegal.

We've marked some of our actions as "**MEDIA FRIENDLY**," which means they might be of interest to journalists in your area. Chapter 38, Get Media Attention, explains how to make your pitch and get coverage.

The Internet has made participating in the electoral process much easier—from registering to vote to keeping track of issues and candidates. We've highlighted some of the best—and truly awesome—resources on the Web. But there's still plenty in this book for people without computers, including some of the most effective actions, which have nothing to do with the Internet.

And if our suggestions don't satisfy you, you can find lots more to do—as well as information about where to obtain stuff we describe—in the "resources" section of each chapter. For any fundraising activity, first identify the organization that you want to help and ask that group for the rules that apply to contributions to it (or expenditures on its behalf). We've referred you to lots of great organizations, many of which educate citizens about important issues, including George W. Bush's destructive policies, but do not take partisan positions.

We emphasize that you should download, copy, and distribute voter registration forms from the Federal Election Commission (fec.gov. votregis/vr.htm) and mail-in ballot request the forms from your state's election office (nased.org/statelinks.org). We suggest that you obtain (from showgeorgethedoor.org) a holder for these forms, allowing you to offer them to people at any counter.

To inspire action, we've also included a memorable Bush quote at the end of each chapter.

A Popular Uprising

For some people, supporting the Democrat will feel just great. For others, such as disillusioned Republicans (who don't like Democrats) or former Nader voters (who don't like Democrats but won't vote for Nader again for fear of tipping the election), casting a ballot for the Democrat will require the use of some powerful nose clips. So be it.

Buy silver or traditional flesh-colored nose clips at HoldYourNose AndVote.org, and wear them proudly around your neck. We authors are both independents. The object of this book is to help vote Bush out. The only way to do that is to vote the Democrat in. That's why we list Democratic Party organizations as Resources. But we are not Democrats. It's a fine line, but we thought we had to scrawl it.

We need to set aside any differences we might have and stand up and say to our fellow citizens and to the rest of the world that Bush does not represent all of us. By raising the visibility of our individual and collective opposition to Bush, we will embolden others and help manifest a popular uprising for change.

The Action that Matters Most

To make it happen, it all comes down to this: we need to get people to vote—the ones who say it's hopeless and meaningless, the ones who are too busy at their jobs or fixing the roof or trying to find a boyfriend or girlfriend or taking care of the kids. We need to take back our country.

We wish it went without saying that everyone who reads this book will vote, but this isn't the case. Some of the people you'd think most likely to vote don't. Research shows that *donors* to liberal activist organizations aren't voting at any higher rate than the rest of the population, which is about 50 percent.

That's right. If you and your friend are Sierra Club members, chances are that only one of you votes.

So whatever you do, VOTE. In most states, you can do it from the comfort of your own home via mail-in ballot. And get your friends to vote. And tell them to get their friends to vote, and our network will grow and our voices will be heard.

Our Power Versus Theirs

Bush's supporters may have money and influence on their side, but we've got the inspiration, the heart, and more people. This book is intended to help you see the full range of possibilities for activating everyone who wants to vote Bush out on November 2. It's up to all of us to build a broad, unrelenting movement that will sweep basic decency and compassion into the White House.

P.S. To get in touch with us, visit showgeorgethedoor.org.

—**Ben Cohen and Jason Salzman**

Part I

50 WAYS TO SHOW GEORGE THE DOOR

★ TOP TEN LIST ★

1. REGISTER PEOPLE (INCLUDING YOURSELF) TO VOTE

Only about half of the citizens who are eligible to vote in our country actually bother to do it. And those who tend not to vote—the poor and disenfranchised—have the most to lose if Bush is re-elected. Registering people to vote is one of the simplest, most important actions anybody can take in the name of regime change at home.

You're thinking, "Who's got time to sit at a little table outside the Post Office and ask people to register to vote? And who wants to?"

You don't. And you don't have to. The Internet has made voter registration amazingly easy.

All you have to do is visit any of the nonpartisan voter registration Web sites listed below, like yourvotematters.org, declareyourself.com or rockthevote.org and follow the instructions. After answering a few basic questions and clicking your mouse a dozen times, you print out a form that's ready for your signature. Sign it, date it, and mail it to the address listed. All you need is a computer with a printer, a pen, and a stamp. The whole process takes less than ten minutes. (Don't make the common mistake of forgetting to sign the form, date it, or mail with a stamp.)

If needed, you can update your voter registration information on many of these same Web sites. You also can print out copies of the form to hand out to others. (Download the form from fec.gov.votreg-is/vr.htm.)

Online voter registration sites also have a "Tell Your Friends" page. Enter your friends' e-mail addresses and they will receive an e-mail explaining how easy it is to register to vote and where they can do it. Then you can phone your friends and tell them they have no excuse not to register immediately. Make sure to follow up before Election Day and remind them to actually vote, too. For voter registration deadlines, see Part 3, Voter Registration (and Mail-in Ballot) Resources and Deadlines.

But Internet-based voter registration isn't for everybody. *In fact, by far the best way to register many types of potential voters, like low-income people, is to greet them face-to-face, discuss the issues, and help them fill out the forms—and then get in touch again to reinforce your previous conversation and, later, to make sure they receive and complete a mail-in ballot or get to the polls.* A large number of partisan and nonpartisan organizations are doing exactly this. It's easy to contact them and get involved in their efforts. (For a list of them with phone numbers, see Chapter 5, Help Defeat Bush in Swing States (Even if You Don't Live in One) and Chapter 6, Educate People About an Issue You Care About—and Register Them to Vote.)

Also, the voter registration Web sites listed below steer you to voter registration activities in your community that, while more time consuming, are more effective in reaching many potential voters.

As you approach people about registering to vote—either in person or online—keep in mind that many people don't like divulging that they are not registered. So don't ask them directly. Just say that you are registering people, and ask if you can help them register without putting them on the spot.

Keep in mind that voter participation by those aged eighteen–twenty-four is in the 15 percent range and shrinking. The turnout rate at the bottom of the income scale is only half that at the top.

 for practical, concerned, and busy people.

E-mail the note below to all your e-mail contacts in your address book, urging them to spread the word about how easy it is to register to vote via the Internet:

Subject: Help Vote Bush Out

Hi,

Do you know how easy it is to register to vote via the Internet? All you have to do is visit a nonpartisan Web site like yourvotematters.com, sponsored by Working Assets Long Distance, and follow the simple directions. In a few minutes, you can print out the fully completed form. Sign it, date it, and mail it in—and you're registered.

If you are already registered, please forward this e-mail to anyone who may not be. Thanks.

 for anti-Bush patriots with time to spare.

Find ways to reach out beyond your circle of friends. Most people who are registered to vote know others who are also registered. What can you do, if you are in this category and you want to have a greater impact?

° You can join the voter registration campaigns of one of the groups listed in Chapter 5, Help Defeat Bush in Swing States (Even if You Don't Live in One) and Chapter 6, Educate People About an Issue You Care About-and Register Them to Vote.

° Work within any institution that you are a part of, whether it's a business, government agency, nonprofit group or volunteer association. Do an inventory of the institution to ensure that voter registration and vote-by-mail material is available everywhere possible. You can: 1) put registration forms in the lobby, on the counter, near the cash register, or anywhere prominent, 2) insert registration information in publications, and 3) place registration links on Web sites. (To get voter registration forms, see Resources below. For vote-by-mail request forms see the next chapter and visit fed.gov/votregis/vr.htm.com and to get a brochure holder for voter registration forms and mail-in-ballot request forms, visit showgeorgethedoor.org. To get a voter registration banner for your Web site, visit declareyourself.com/press_banners.htm.)

 for the anybody-but-Bush guerilla.

MEDIA FRIENDLY: Operate a pink lemonade stand for voter registration. Guerillas are drawn to media-savvy activist groups like Code Pink (codepink.org), which is currently collecting pink slips (the lingerie variety) with anti-Bush sentiments written on them from people across America. They plan to display the pink slips in Washington, D.C., to highlight Bush's unemployment mess. Code Pink is also operating pink lemonade stands for voter registration, complete with voter registration forms and mail-in ballot request forms. They plan to offer the lemonade in areas with high concentrations of young women. Find out from Code Pink whether there's one happening near you—or start your own. Set up your stand in front of a college, church, or school and serve the people you want to register.

Bushism

"The great thing about America is everybody should vote."
—George W. Bush, Austin, Texas, December 8, 2000

Resources

How to Obtain Blank Voter Registration Forms to Copy and Hand Out. Visit the Federal Election Commission Web site at fec.gov/votregis/vr.htm. Read through the introduction and click on "For Public Use" at the bottom. This leads you to the federal government's National Voter Registration Form, plus lots of background information on state rules. Print the form (pages 4–7) and scroll down to find the proper address for submission in your state. You can then add the proper address on the reverse side of the form, make as many copies as you can afford, and hand them out at will. Information on where to submit the forms is on the Web site—as are the variations on the rules by some states. Consider submitting—either by mail or in person—completed forms on behalf of the folks who fill them out. If you do this, make sure they sign and date them. (The form is not accepted in New Hampshire and Wyoming, which have their own forms, and North Dakota, which does not require voter registration at all.) In most cases, a person registering to vote for the first time will have to provide identification *when they actually vote*—unless a copy of an ID is submitted with the voter registration form.

How to Register to Vote via the Internet. The following are just a few of many Web sites that offer online voter registration. They are nonpartisan, which means that they offer equal opportunity voter registration to people of all political stripes, including Bush stripes. As explained above, all you have to do is fill out the form online, print it out, sign it, date it, address an envelope, find a stamp, and mail it.

☞ Declare Yourself (declareyourself.org) is a bit difficult to navigate but worth the extra effort because it has excellent resources on election issues, including a great tool to order mail-in ballots from most states. The nonpartisan site is oriented toward young voters.

☞ League of Women Voters (lwv.org) has excellent step-by-step instructions that walk you through the registration process, in addition to offering guides you can purchase that make the experience very easy to understand. It's in Spanish and English, and is nonpartisan.

☛ Click on the voter registration link on the home page of the nonpartisan Rock the Vote (rockthevote.org). This site aims for young, urban, music- and media-savvy hipsters.

☛ The "Faith in Action" section of the nonpartisan Sojourners Web site (sojo.net) features the motto "Register, Pray, Vote," and offers a handy voter registration tool, which allows you to register yourself and e-mail friends to encourage them to register as well.

☛ Your Vote Matters (yourvotematters.org) offers an excellent, nonpartisan voter registration form, provides a way to send voter registration information to e-mail contacts, and gives other options for civic participation and voter registration. The sponsor is Working Assets Long Distance.

How to Obtain a Voter Registration Form by Phone. If you want to order a voter registration form by phone, see Part 3, Voter Registration (and Mail-in Ballot) Resources and Deadlines. Or for nonpartisan election-related information, call Project Vote Smart's voter research hotline (888-868-3762).

How to Get Involved with Organizations Conducting On-the-Ground Voter Registration Drives. For information on organizations conducting nonpartisan on-the-ground voter registration drives, see Chapter 6, Educate People About an Issue You Care About—and Register Them to Vote. For voter registration in swing states, see Chapter 5, Help Defeat Bush in Swing States (Even if You Don't Live in One). For more information on the Democratic Party's projects on voter registration, visit democrats.org.

How to Find Voter Registration Deadlines. See Part 3, Voter Registration (and Mail-in Ballot) Resources and Deadlines.

2. *VOTE BY MAIL-IN BALLOT*

Voting by mail is changing U.S. elections. In some states, like Oregon, most people already send in ballots by mail, and the number of people doing it has been increasing around the country.

Even if you won't be out of town on Election Day, there are a bunch of good reasons to vote by mail-in ballot if it's an option in your state.

The best reason is that campaigns with successful vote-by-mail programs increase voter turnout for their side. Why? Voting by mail is easy—not to mention the fact that a car accident, bad weather, a child-care crisis, a fight with the boyfriend, even death won't stop you from voting if you've already voted by mail. (Our lawyer requires us to tell you that that was a joke.)

The trouble is, the Republicans have utilized mail-in ballots much more effectively than the Democrats. So they've not only turned out more voters with mail-in ballots, but fewer of their supporters waste time standing in line at the polls on Election Day—and instead, they're free to help get voters to the polls.

More of us should use mail-in ballots, too. Essentially, mail-in ballots are a convenience for those who might be inclined not to vote for whatever reason—or those who want to maximize their time to mobilize voters on Election Day.

Many states refer to mail-in ballots as "absentee ballots." But in most states, you do not have to be absent, on vacation, or otherwise unable to get to the polls to use an absentee ballot. In other words, you can treat an "absentee ballot" like a "mail-in ballot."

In fact, in most states, it's as easy to request a mail-in ballot via the Internet as it is to register to vote online. Simply visit declareyourself.com, a nonpartisan voter registration Web site. On the left hand side of the home page, click on "Vote Today!!! How? Absentee Ballot." Then, enter your state or ZIP code, and follow the on-screen directions, which culminate in your printing out a completed form, signing it, addressing an envelope to the appropriate election office in your state (the address is provided), and stamping and mailing the letter. You will then receive your ballot in the mail, and you can vote in bed if you want. Just remember to mail in your ballot by the deadline. *IF YOU ARE A FIRST-TIME VOTER, YOU'LL NEED TO INCLUDE A COPY OF A FORM OF IDENTIFICATION WITH YOUR MAIL-IN BALLOT WHEN YOU SEND IT.*

If you reside in Arizona, Arkansas, Illinois, Kentucky, Louisiana, Maine, Nevada, North Carolina, South Carolina, or Washington, you cannot fill out the mail-in ballot request form and print it out via declareyourself.com. Instead, declareyourself.com will lead you to the Web site of your state's election office, where you'll find the appropriate procedures for requesting a mail-in ballot. Or you can visit nased.org/statelinks.htm and click on your state. Or check out activoteamerica.com.

The rules about when and how to request a mail-in ballot vary by state. In Oregon, for example, mail-in ballots are the primary means of voting. In other states, it's not an option unless there's a demonstrable need, like illness. And some states require that you request your mail-in ballot at least three weeks or more in advance. Check with your Secretary of State's office to determine what options are available to you. For contact information and the rules, see Part 3, "Voter Registration (and Mail-in Ballot) Resources and Deadlines.

Remember to sign, date, and mail (with stamp) both the request form and the actual ballot.

 for the practical, concerned, and busy person.

E-mail this note to your friends, urging them to request a mail-in ballot:

Subject: Join Me in Voting Bush Out

Hi,

Everyone who wants to show George the door should request a mail-in ballot, so you can avoid waiting in line on Election Day—and so that no mishap prevents you from voting against Bush. If you want, you could dedicate the time you would have spent voting—or more time if you can—on Election Day to getting people to vote.

I just ordered my mail-in ballot. It's easy. Just visit declareyour self.com, a Web site sponsored by Norman Lear and others. Click on "Vote Today!!! How? Absentee Ballot" and follow the easy steps. Or call 888-868-3762 for information. Don't forget to sign and date your form before mailing it in.

Do it in the name of regime change at home, and please forward this message. Thanks.

 for anti-Bush patriots with time to spare.

Submit request forms for mail-in ballots on behalf of others. Print your state's mail-in ballot request form from the Web at nased.org/statelinks.htm, make copies of it, and hand the forms out at any large gathering of like-minded political folk. For example, you could distribute them at your place of worship or your kid's soccer game. If you do this, consider suggesting to people that if they fill out the request forms immediately, you will submit them on their behalf. If you can, follow-up and remind them to mail in their actual ballots once they arrive. Have voter registration forms on hand as well (they're available at fec.gov/votregis/vr.htm).

 for the anybody-but-Bush guerilla.

Make sure guerillas and others request, get, and submit mail-in ballots. With your mail-in ballot, you can vote from anywhere you want and at any time of day even in the middle of the night. That's good for guerillas. It's also good for other people who work on vampire time like college students, artists, musicians, dancers, and others. Give mail-in ballot request forms to people like this at concerts, bars, raves, college campuses, and elsewhere. Follow-up to make sure they fill out the forms and vote.

Bushism

"As people do better, they start voting like Republicans ... unless they have too much education and vote Democratic, which proves there can be too much of a good thing."
—Karl Rove, as quoted in "Bush's Trillions," by Nicholas Lemann, *The New Yorker*, February 19 and 26, 2001

Resources

How to Request a Mail-In Ballot via the Internet. Visit declareyourself.com, a nonpartisan voter registration Web site. On the left hand side of the home page, click on "Vote Today!!! How? Absentee Ballot." Follow the on-screen directions. If you are a first time voter, submit a copy of a form of with your ballot when you mail it in.

For deadlines and rules for submitting mail-in ballots in your state, see Part 3, Voter Registration (and Mail-in Ballot) Deadlines and Resources. Also visit nased.org/statelinks.htm and click on your state.

How to Obtain a Blank Mail-In Ballot Request Form for Copying and Handing Out. Visit the official federal government Web site at firstgov.com/Citizen/ Topics/Voting.shtml and click the "Register to Vote and Go Vote" link. This will direct you to the bottom of the page, where absentee or mail-in ballots are discussed. Click on the link appropriate for your situation (in or out of the country), and you will be directed to a page with a link for the election office of every state and American Samoa, Virgin Islands, Guam, and Washington, D.C. Browse the Web site and try to locate your state's absentee, early voting, or mail-in ballot request form. A few states require that you call or write the office, using a phone number or address on the Web site, to get the appropriate form.

To Obtain a Mail-In Ballot by Phone. See Part 3: Voter Registration (and Mail-in Ballot) Resources and Deadlines for the phone number of your state's election office. Call and ask for a mail-in ballot request form.

Check activoteamerica.com for more information about mail-in voting procedures and the voter registration process. Click on "Resources."

Another way to find out about mail-in ballots in your state is to call your local Democratic Party Campaign office. Most political campaigns put major resources into getting people to vote early, if it's an option, or by mail-in ballot in order to make sure they vote and to free them up to mobilize other voters on Election Day. So contact your local Democratic Party office for information: www.democrats.org/states/.

In an effort to save time and money, some states offer One-Stop voting. This process allows eligible voters to request an absentee ballot in person and cast their ballot at the same time. Voters are still required to meet pre-established absentee voter qualifications. Contact your state's election office to determine if this option is available to you. For contact information, see Part 3, Voter Registration (and Mail-in Ballot) Resources and Deadlines. Or call Project Vote Smart's research hotline (888-868-3762) for nonpartisan information.

3. PETS FOR REGIME CHANGE

Animals get people's attention. For proof, just flip on the local TV news, which finds the most popular eye candy out there and broadcasts it day after day after day. You'll see the polar bear's birthday party at the zoo, eleven kittens in a baby stroller, the lizard in the drainpipe, and so much more that you will soon be dreaming about animals, if you aren't already.

Animals have the right mix of cute and unpredictable behavior that gets noticed.

Animals also bring people together. Neighbors converse while their pets pee together on a tree or lamppost. People seem to be at their friendliest when walking the dog. So, your challenge is to enlist animals in your campaign to defeat George Bush.

You may ask yourself, "Will my pet want to help?" Don't worry. While a few pets may be swayed by Dubya's monkey-like looks, most are so mad about his farm policies and lack of support for the middle class family (home of many, many pets) that they want to do their part. Live animals, as opposed to stuffed ones or costumes, work best. Pets are the obvious choice but not necessarily the only option.

As you imagine how to involve animals—preferably manageable ones—in the anti-Bush campaign, be aware that your activities may draw protests from animal rights organizations, particularly if you do not handle your live beings with care, which you should.

 *for practical, concerned, and busy people.*

Decorate your pet's leash with a "Bite Bush" button. Take advantage of the warm feelings that pets generate to talk politics with your neighbors. A "Bite Bush" button on your dog's leash gives you the chance to strike up a conversation with most anyone—all while you are walking the dog, which you have to do anyway. (Get your "Bite Bush" button at buttonshack.com.)

Waggles Wants to Vote Bush Out. *Photo credit: Mark Manger*

Give your pet a temporary new name. At the dog park, dog's names are a big topic of discussion. Tell curious strangers your dog is named something political, like "Big Oil" or "Hanging Chad." This creates a chance to talk about an issue you care about, and it might have legs; your listener might think it's funny, and tell his friends and family about the weird dog name. This works for other pets, too.

 for anti-Bush patriots with time to spare.

Dress your pet in anti-Bush clothes. Find an anti-Bush knitter who will create a "Stop Bush" sweater for your doggie. There are also easier routes to go with this. Wrap a bandana around the neck of your furry friend with "Vote" written on it.

Drop leaflets and give out stickers while you walk the dog.
Walking the dog is a great time to pass out voter registration forms
and mail-in ballot request forms—as well as "Show George the
Door" stickers (showgeorgethedoor.org). If you walk your dog daily
anyway, why not select a couple days to drop off leaflets and talk to
your neighbors about the need for regime change at home? It's
much better to actually talk to people, rather than just leave a
leaflet at the door, but do what you can.

 for the anybody-but-Bush guerilla.

**MEDIA FRIENDLY: I'm hopping mad at Bush and I plan to
vote.** Guerillas love shock and awe, as long as it's not the bombing
variety. So, they love to do silly things with animals, like bunny rab-

 bits. Here's what you do: Recruit a
couple friends and go to the pet store
and buy a couple of large rabbits—or
find someone who has pet bunnies
that they will lend you. Also, get
bunny masks for your group. (See
"Resources" below.) Then, make large
signs that read, "I'm Hopping Mad at
Bush and I Plan to Vote." With sign
and rabbits in hand, go to a busy park
or mall. Put the rabbits beside you,
preferably on a leash but in a cage if
you must. Put on your mask, stand
next to the bunnies, hold up your sign,
and hop as long as your legs will hold
out. Hop in shifts for greater impact.

Express yourself with the help of your pets.

Credit: Jesse Mangerson

MEDIA FRIENDLY: An animal in a wagon. Take advantage of
the cultural obsession with animals by renting an unusual one. Put
it in a wagon and pull it around your city with a sign like, "We Need
a Friendlier Animal in the White House. Register to Vote."

Bushism

"Then I went for a run with the other dog and just walked. And I started thinking about a lot of things. I was able to— I can't remember what it was. Oh, the inaugural speech, started thinking through that."—George W. Bush, *U.S. News and World Report*, January 22, 2001

Resources

Animals: If you need to borrow an animal for this action, there are plenty of local organizations you can contact. Start with any of the state farmers unions (nfu.org) to be put in touch with a family farmer who may be on your side. Also try animal rescue shelters, petting zoos, and 4-H organizations.

"Bite Bush" Buttons: buttonshack.com.

To obtain mail-in ballot request forms for your state, visit nased.org/statelinks.htm.

For voter registration forms for your state, visit fec.gov/votregis/vr.htm.

4. GIFTS FOR THE ELECTION SEASON

As November 2 rapidly approaches, more and more beautiful election-related gifts are flooding the market. As you'll see below, there are goodies for every type of person.

Consider taking advantage of an upcoming occasion, like a birthday or anniversary, to give some of this inspired stuff to loved ones or even not-so-loved ones. In fact, why not dream up an excuse to give away this stuff? (or use our excuses, listed after the gift ideas below.)

Gift ideas for different personality types.

"Liar, Liar, Pants on Fire" Doll.

Photo credit: showgeorgethedoor.org

☞ For the doll lover: "Liar, Liar, Pants on Fire" doll. (pantsonfire.net)

☞ For the guy's guy with nude pinups in the garage: A "Babes Against Bush" calendar featuring semi-nude anti-Bushies. (babesagainstbush.com)

☞ For card players: "War Profiteers" playing cards (ruckus.org) or "Pack of Lies." (truemajorityACTION.org)

☞ For the person with no sense of humor: A donation in his or her name to the Democratic National Committee. (democrats.org)

☞ For the music lover: CD of anti-Bush parodies (dimpledchad.net) or Rock Against Bush compilation CD. (fatwreck.com)

☞ For the angry psychotic who hates everything on the right: A dart board and an Ann Coulter doll to hang in front of the bull's-eye. (dutchguard.com)

☞ For the minimalist: A tasteful slip of paper, reminding them to vote.

☞ For the recently deceased: Send money in memory of the deceased to your favorite progressive organization.

☞ For the eighteen-year-old birthday girl or boy: A voter registration form.

☞ For the Disney liberal: Bushocchio, the inflatable doll that tells the story of a Bush, dressed in his flight suit, with a giant nose. (seeyageorge.com)

☞ For the sweet tooth: A plate of cookies you just made with your Democratic donkey cookie cutter. (tigereyedesign.com)

☞ For the retired librarian who always corrects your grammar and generally votes Republican: A "Presidential (Mis) Speak 2004 Calendar": the Very Curious Language of George W. Bush. (bushcalendar.com)

☞ For the person who appreciates potty humor, like Jason's brother Charlie: Wipe-Bush-Out-of-Office toilet paper (whatpresident.com) or a G.W. Bush doll whose finger you pull for hours of lowbrow amusement. (prankplace.com)

☞ For the witty poet: "Jail to the Thief" T-shirt. (fringefolk.com)

☞ For the classic poster fan: "I Only Joined for the College Money" poster. (democracylost.com)

☞ For the person who talks endlessly about how offensive Bush is but does nothing about it: This book!

☞ For the coffee achiever: Mug reading "Proud Member of the Vast Left Wing Majority." (smirkingchimp.com)

☞ For the moral relativist: "No One Died When Clinton Lied" bumper sticker. (seeyageorge.com)

☞ For the snail-mail dinosaur: Envelope labels. (powerstickers.com)

☛ For the non-Atkins gourmet: "Bread Not Bombs" cutting board. (donnellycolt.com/catalog/fun.html)

☛ For those who are too young to talk: "Uncle Sam Wants You" bib. (cafeshops.com/warposter/62216)

☛ For everyone you know: Voter registration and mail-in ballot request forms.

☛ For travelers: Absentee ballot applications.

Include voter registration and mail-in ballot request forms with all gifts.

Excuses for giving presents between now and Election Day:

May 31:   Memorial Day

June 2:   Full Moon

June 14:   Flag Day

June 20:   Father's Day and Summer Solstice

June 30:   Deadline for U.S. to hand sovereignty back to Iraq

July 1:   Canada Day

July 4:   Independence Day

July 6:   George W. Bush's Birthday

Aug. 2:   Three months until Election Day

Aug. 12:   International Youth Day

Aug. 18:   Bad Poetry Day

Aug. 21:   National Forgiveness Day

Sept. 6:   Labor Day

Sept 12:   National Grandparents' Day

Sept. 17:   Citizenship Day

Oct. 2:   One month until Election Day

Oct. 22:   National Nut Day

Oct. 24:   United Nations Day

Oct. 31:   Halloween

fon pnactical, concenned, and busy people.

Give at least one gift to a swing voter you love. Select a holiday (or an excuse) and a gift from the above list, and give an on-message gift to the right person.

 fon anti-Bush patniots with time to spane.

Each month, present a different loved one with a gift. Each month between now and the election, pick the right left person, and give him or her a gift that will count toward the greatest gift of all: a new president.

 fon the anybody-but-Bush guenilla.

Be a capitalist for a day. If they had taken a different path in life, most guerillas would have been premier (and rich) capitalists—figuring out the most creative ways to sell stuff at the best prices. Here's a chance to put your repressed capitalist skills to work. Buy five "Liar, Liar, Pants on Fire" dolls from showgeorgethedoor.org and hawk them any way you can, spreading the anti-Bush (and pro-vote) word as you go.

Bushism

"Well, it's an unimaginable honor to be the president during the Fourth of July of this country. It means what these words say, for starters. The great inalienable rights of our country. We're blessed with such values for America. And I—it's— I'm a proud man to be the nation based upon such wonderful values."—George W. Bush, visiting the Jefferson Memorial, Washington, D.C., July 2, 2001

Resources

The Web sites for many gifts are listed above, but check out democrats.com. It has a clearinghouse of electoral gifts.

5. HELP DEFEAT BUSH IN SWING STATES
(EVEN IF YOU DON'T LIVE IN ONE)

Some states, like Texas, will almost certainly vote for Bush in November. Others, like Maryland, will almost certainly vote for the Democrat. Other states where neither Bush nor John Kerry has a clear advantage are called the swing states. Depending on whom you're listening to, there are between fifteen and thirty swing states where either candidate could win. The votes in these states will probably decide the election. (See Part 2, Election Primer: Swing States, Electoral College, and More.)

So, should everyone dedicate *all* their energy to defeating Bush in swing states? The answer is no.

First, we won't know which states are the key swing states until the months just prior to the election. And in the end, some states always surprise the "experts."

Also, the momentum and visibility of the anti-Bush campaign across the country has an impact on the swing states. For example, if Bush is drawing huge crowds of protestors as he campaigns and the Democrat is greeted with throngs of supporters, this will make national news and the impact will be felt and seen (literally) in the swing states.

And in the bigger picture, stopping Bush and company includes winning close Senate and House races that aren't in swing states. This is particularly important if Bush wins again.

So, we should try to do both: help out if we can in swing states and take action to show George the door in our local communities, even if they are not in swing states.

This chapter focuses on the swing state part.

A number of progressive organizations are dedicating all or most of their election resources on likely swing states. And they are not doing it by bombarding America's living rooms with negative advertising. Instead, they'll be walking through neighborhoods, knocking on doors, and registering people to vote, particularly low-income and disenfranchised folks who've been hurt the most by Bush yet who typically vote least. The goal is to increase the number of Democratic voters who make it to the polls.

This can work because the number of nonvoters who are on our side (like low-income and disenfranchised citizens, unmarried women, and young people) is much larger than those who would support Bush if they voted, and once they are registered they can make a difference.

While experts differ on exactly which states will turn out to be swing states in the November election, the following is a list of states commonly identified as swing: Arizona, Arkansas, Florida, Iowa, Maine, Michigan, Minnesota, Missouri, Nevada, New Hampshire, New Mexico, Ohio, Oregon, Pennsylvania, Washington, West Virginia, and Wisconsin.

You can help register and mobilize voters in swing states, even if you don't live in one. Here's a list of organizations that will be looking for volunteers:

☛ **America Coming Together** (act4victory.org, 202-974-8360) is the largest of the swing state projects, focusing on voter outreach and registration in seventeen "battleground" states. Sign up for e-mail updates on the ACT Web site.

☛ **America Votes** (americavotes.org, 202-974-8330) is an inspiring coalition of dozens of national organizations—from the AFL-CIO to the Sierra Club, representing over twenty million Americans—that will work *together* in swing states, using the latest techniques to register and mobilize voters on issues they care about.[1] They will create joint state plans for voter outreach, so dif-

---

[1] Some of the organizations listed are nonpartisan, which means they do not have a position on whether Bush should be re-elected. Instead, they educate citizens on important policy positions of Bush and other politicians.

ferent progressive groups don't waste time contacting the same
people over and over again. Sign up on their Web site to receive
action opportunities. Also, in its "Meet the Organizations" section,
the America Votes Web site lists over twenty organizations that are
part of the coalition. Peruse this list to see if these coalition members have an affiliate in your area. If they do, call and find out
what volunteer opportunities are available and, specifically, if they
have programs (phone banking, canvassing, fundraising, etc.) in
your area that are directed at the battleground states.

☛ **Association of Community Organizations for Reform Now**
(acorn.org, 877-55ACORN) is looking for volunteers living in or
willing to travel to battleground states for voter registration
drives during the summer or for voter mobilization during the
week prior to the election. Training will be provided upon arrival
in a swing state. Those interested should send an e-mail to
ACORN at polnat@acorn.org. Put "2004 volunteer" in the subject line.

☛ **Citizen Action**'s (volunteer2004.org) affiliates in New York and
elsewhere are organizing volunteers from around the country to
make a difference in swing states. Visit volunteer2004.org for
ways to volunteer from your home state (by making phone calls,
for example) or to travel to swing states throughout the summer
and fall. There will be organized bus trips from New York, New
Jersey, and other states to battleground states for voter registration and mobilization.

☛ **Democratic National Committee** (dnc.org, 202-863-8000) will
send you action alerts and information. Sign up on its Web site
and also check out its election blog, "Kicking Ass." You should be
on both the national and state affiliates' e-mail lists.

☛ Sign up on **Good Government's Swing State Project** (goodgov-
ernment.org/swingstate/index.htm), chaired by Granny D, to
make a commitment to be a "swing state volunteer" and receive
action options. Also check the site for a discussion board and
downloadable flyers and leaflets.

☛ **Mainstreet Moms Oppose Bush** (MMOB) will e-mail you "bite-sized" actions, particularly focused on turning out the "mom vote" in swing states. To join, send an e-mail to matson8@earth-link.net.

☛ **MoveOn.org PAC**, the Web-based activist group, is already offering its members the opportunity to contribute toward advertising campaigns in swing states. MoveOn.org (voter fund) posts proposed ads on its Web site, and members decide which ads they like and whether they want to make a contribution toward running the ads. MoveOn.org PAC may organize "phone banks" in your area where you can make calls to voters in swing states, using MoveOn.org's talking points—or you may be able to get a list of names and make calls independently. To learn more about what you can do, sign up at MoveOn.org.

☛ **The NAACP Voter Fund** (naacpnvf.org, 202-898-0960) will mobilize and educate voters in swing states.

☛ **Partnership for America's Families** (americasfamilies.org, 202-974-8300) is registering women, people of color, and working families in battleground states. Sign up to receive action suggestions.

☛ **TrueMajorityACTION.org**, (212-243-3416) another Web-based activist group, will offer its members resources to organize house parties, lectures, and other activities in support of regime change—with an emphasis on swing states. A planned video—which could be screened at house parties and other events—will feature ten ways to make a difference in the election. Celebrities in the video will demonstrate how each action is done.

☛ **Twenty-First Century Democrats** (21stcenturydems.org, 202-626-5620) focuses on providing training for campaign organizers.

☛ **Voices for Working Families** (voicesforworkingfamilies.org, 202-974-8320) works with volunteers in sixteen battleground states to register women and people of color to vote. One program called "Bring Your Daughter to Work" aims to get young people involved.

 for practical, concerned, and busy people.

Donate money to one of the groups listed above. It's about as easy and practical as it gets. And tell your friends about them. (Most of the Web sites have a "tell-a-friend" feature.)

 for anti-Bush patriots with time to spare.

Sign up and take action. Sign up with one of the organizations listed above and receive swing state action alerts. Set aside volunteer time as the opportunities present themselves this summer and fall.

 for the anybody-but-Bush guerilla.

Go to a swing state. Guerillas like the hands-on approach. So, sign up with one of the groups above and plan a trip to your favorite swing state.

Bushism

"The important question is, how many hands have I shaked?"
—George W. Bush, answering a question about why he hadn't spent more time in New Hampshire prior to the 2000 election, as quoted in the *New York Times*, October 23, 1999

Resources

For more information, see Part 2, An Election Primer: Swing States, the Electoral College, and More.

Another way to make a difference is to educate voters about issues, not candidates, in swing states and elsewhere. Many nonpartisan groups have launched programs to register new voters who care about jobs, the environment, women's rights, and other causes. And many of these groups are looking for volunteers to work in battleground states and elsewhere. See Chapter 6, Educate People About an Issue You Care About—and Register Them to Vote.

As Election Day approaches and it becomes clearer which states will be the most critical swing states, many organizations will be offering specific actions to make a difference. See Chapter 49, Stay Informed About Late-Breaking Actions and Issues.

You could also connect with Democratic Campaign offices (democrats.org, 202-863-8000) in swing states. Protesting Bush when he comes to your state can affect voters in swing states—because demonstrations can get national media coverage. See Chapter 16, When Bush and Company Visit, Protest!

6. EDUCATE PEOPLE ABOUT AN ISSUE YOU CARE ABOUT—AND REGISTER THEM TO VOTE

To make the complex political world manageable, we focus on a handful of issues that we care a lot about. We track these issues and watch what political candidates say about them.

For example, as authors, we both closely follow the debate about the Pentagon budget. We believe that cutting funding for expensive Cold War–era weapons systems is the best way to begin solving our social problems—both at home and abroad. This is because wasteful militarism drains so much of America's resources and those of the world. Visit TrueMajority.org/oreo, to see Ben use Oreo cookies to show what we could do for ourselves and the planet by trimming Pentagon spending by just 15 percent.

Anyway, that's our issue. Yours might be the environment, choice, livable wage, gay rights, or something else.

Many organizations have launched campaigns to reach out to voters who care about these issues, register them to vote, and get them to the polls.

Check out the Web sites of the groups below and if you are interested in joining one or more, contact them to find out if they are active in your area. These are just samples of the groups working on issue-oriented voter registration and education. There are many more out there, including lots of state and local groups. Many groups listed are strictly nonpartisan, and have no position on whether George be shown the door, but they are raising awareness of important issues.

African-American Issues

☞ **A. Philip Randolph Institute** (apri.org, 202-289-2774) engages in nonpartisan activities to involve more African Americans and trade unionists in politics.

☞ **The NAACP** (naacp.org, 410-521-4939) is running a nonpartisan "Voter Empowerment Program" to increase the involvement of African Americans in the electoral process. The Web site has a step-by-step guide for approaching people and asking them to register to vote.

Environmental Issues

☞ **Clean Water Action** (cleanwateraction.org, 202-895-0420) works on a wide range of environmental issues and mobilizes its members in support of environmental candidates.

☞ **League of Conservation Voters** (lcv.org, 202-785-8683) publishes a Presidential Report Card and works to elect environment-friendly candidates.

☞ **Sierra Club's** (sierraclub.org, 202-547-1141) Environmental Voter Education Campaign plans to mobilize and train thousands of volunteers prior to the 2004 election.

Gay and Lesbian Issues

☞ **Human Rights Campaign** (hrc.org, 202-628-4160) provides candidate voting records and public education.

☞ **National Gay and Lesbian Task Force** (ngltf.org, 202-393-5177) works at the state and local level on gay and lesbian issues.

☞ **National Stonewall Democrats** (stonewalldemocrats.org, 202-625-1382) has local chapters that educate and mobilize voters.

Labor Issues

☞ **AFL-CIO** (aflcio.org, 202-637-5000) has various member unions, including AFSCME (afscme.org), SEIU (seiu.org), the

Teamsters (teamster.org), the NEA (nea.org), and others with voter mobilization programs. (AFSCME and SEIU have particularly good resources on their Web sites.)

Latino Issues

☞ **Mexican American Legal Defense Fund** (maldef.org, 213-629-2512) enhances Latino influence by nurturing more political involvement by Latinos.

☞ **Moving America Forward** (hispanicconsultants.com, 202-263-4397) aims to involve more Latinos in the political process.

☞ **Southwest Voter Education Fund** (svrep.org, 800-404-8683) educates Latinos about the Democratic process.

☞ **United States Hispanic Leadership Institute** (ushli.com, 312-427-8683) conducts leadership programs and voter registration in forty states.

Low Income and People of Color Communities

☞ **The Association of Community Organizations for Reform Now** (ACORN) (acorn.org, 202-547-2500) will be registering voters at concerts and in low-income and minority neighborhoods. Saturday canvassing is planned.

☞ **US Action** (usaction.org, 202-624-1730) has thirty-three affiliates, many of which are statewide progressive coalitions and state chapters that register low-income voters.

☞ **Project Vote** (projectvote.org, 800-546-8683) focuses on voter registration and education.

☞ **Center for Community Change** (communitychange.org, 202-342-0519) conducts voter registration.

Peace and Security Issues

☞ **People for the American Way** (pfaw.org, 202-467-4999) defends basic freedoms and promotes voter registration.

☛ **Women Action for New Directions PAC** (wand.org, 781-643-6740) is offering action tips and voter registration information.

Women's Issues

☛ **Feminist Majority Foundation's** (feminist.org, 703-522-2214) nonpartisan "Get Out HER Vote" project will focus on educating and mobilizing voters.

☛ **NARAL Pro-Choice America** (naral.org, 202-973-3000) has numerous state chapters and engages in a wide variety of political work.

☛ **National Organization for Women** (NOW) (now.org, 202-628-8669) has volunteer programs across the country, and an "unmarried women's project."

☛ **Planned Parenthood Action Fund** (ppfa.org, 202-973-4830) runs voter education, registration, and mobilization programs.

Youth Issues

☛ **Voter Virgin's** (votervirgin.com, 866-649-9182) slogan is, "Everybody's Doin' it in '04."

☛ **Center for Public Interest Research's New Voters Project** (newvotersproject.org, 303-573-5885) will engage in nonpartisan voter registration on and off campus.

☛ **Declare Yourself** (declareyourself.com) is a multifaceted campaign to increase voter turnout among young adults.

☛ **PunkVoter** (punkvoter.com) is a coalition of punk bands, musicians, and record labels coming together to oppose Bush.

☛ **Rock the Vote** (rockthevote.org, 202-828-0138) organizes nonpartisan youth voter turnout events.

☛ **Hip Hop Action Summit** (hiphopsummitactionnetwork.org) is dedicated to educate and activate the hip-hop generation on civic participation.

☞ **Youth Vote Coalition** (youthvote.org, 202-783-4751) is a nonpartisan coalition to engage youth in the political process.

Training

☞ In addition to listing its campaign workshops, **Democratic Gain's** (democraticgain.org) Web site lists training conducted nationwide. Check the resources section.

☞ **Emily's List** (emilyslist.org, 202-326-1400) provides training for veteran and rookie politicos. The Web site has a job bank of positions with Democratic campaigns.

☞ **Wellstone Action** (wellstone.org, 651-645-3939) runs "Camp Wellstones" to train activists and campaign volunteers.

 for practical, concerned, and busy people.

Make a donation. It takes just a few minutes to peruse the Web sites of these groups—or call them for information—and make a donation.

 for anti-Bush patriots with time to spare.

Volunteer. Select the issue you want to work on, contact the organization listed, and ask if they need volunteers in your area.

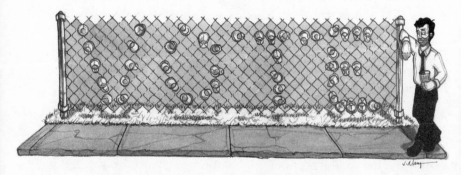

Activists use red, white, and blue cups to spell words, like VOTE, in fences.

Credit: Jesse Mangerson

for the anybody-but-Bush guerilla.

Make a "Vote" sign in a fence using cups. Guerillas are masters at using everyday objects for political enlightenment. Find an agreeable fence in a neighborhood populated by people who will likely vote against Bush. Spell out "VOTE" using red, white, and blue cups. (Remember to clean up after the election.)

Bushism

"Just remember, it's the birds that's supposed to suffer, not the hunter."—George W. Bush to quail hunter Sen. Pete Domenici (R-NM) Roswell, New Mexico, January 22, 2004

Resources

For a list of nonpartisan voter registration campaigns focusing on issues not candidates, visit National Voice (nationalvoice.org), which is a coalition of nonprofit groups working to "maximize public participation in our nation's democratic process." Click on "Voter Projects" to access an extensive list of organizations working on voter-related projects. The "Volunteers" section of the site lists volunteer opportunities on specific dates.

Many nonprofit organizations like many of those listed in this chapter are rightfully concerned about what an organization can legally communicate in an electoral context. For answers, check out *Loud and Clear in the Election Year: Amplifying the Voices of Community Advocates*, edited by Holly Minch with Kim Haddow and Laura Saponara. Available at spinproject.org.

7. HOST A PARTY FOR VOTING, REGISTRATION, OR FUNDRAISING

A standard feature of an election campaign is a "house party." Supporters of a candidate get their friends together, usually in their homes, to learn about a political issue or a candidate, recruit volunteers, donate money, and have fun.

We recommend putting the emphasis on fun, while you also accomplish the serious stuff.

Here are four goals that you might have for your house party, depending on what kind of crowd you run with:

Voter registration: If you think your friends might not be registered, give them voter registration forms at your party. (See Chapter 1, Register People (Including Yourself) to Vote.)

Request mail-in ballots: Consider asking your friends to request a mail-in ballot at your party, so it's easier to vote and they can spend their time on Election Day mobilizing other voters. Give them mail-in ballot request forms and mail them from the party. A follow-up party could be held to fill out and send in the ballots. (See Chapter 2, Vote by Mail-In Ballot.")

Fundraising: One important way we will be able to fight the Bush fundraising machine is one small check at a time. Consider asking your party attendees to give to nonpartisan voter registration campaigns. For a list of groups, see Chapter 6, Educate People About an Issue You Care About—and Register Them to Vote. Or give to the Democrats (democrats.org). If you collect money, make sure you follow the rules applicable to the group receiving the funds.

Get to the polls: Many campaign organizers advise against holding house parties on Election Day because they want every available body working to get voters to the polls. However, if your friends are the kind of sloths who may not make it to the voting booth despite their good intentions, you might want to have a house party on Election Day so you can all head to the polls together. Or, you might hold your party a few days before Election Day and ask all attendees to promise to get at least ten people they know to vote on November 2.

How to pull off an election house party? Organizing one is much like hosting any other social gathering. Here's what you do:

Pick your goals. Choose one or more from the list above, or decide on something else. Make sure you've got voter registration and mail-in ballot request forms. (See Resources below for information on how to get them.)

Decide on entertainment. A house party almost always has some kind of group activity, often followed by discussion. Some options include:

☛ A DVD or video featuring the candidate, available from your local campaign office (find yours at democrats.org or 202-863-8000);

☛ A DVD or video about what you can do to defeat Bush (contact showgeorgethedoor.org.);

☛ A video addressing a key issue in the campaign, like "Uncovered: the Whole Truth About the Iraq War," a film about the lies that were used by Bush to gain support for the war (available from MoveOn.org) or "Unprecedented," about the Florida election fiasco (available from unprecedented.org);

☛ A game like volleyball or croquet, or a theme game like the ones described in the next chapter.

Select a time and date. Weekdays between 5 and 7:30 p.m. are common. If you have invited a speaker, set your time in accordance with his or her schedule.

Select food and beverages. A potluck often works well. Theme dinners are fun. (See examples in the next chapter.)

Develop a guest list. Any number of people will work, but a group between ten and thrity-five is a good target, depending on how much room you have. About a third of the people you invite might actually attend, but you never know.

Pick a location. A house is good because it's personal, but if you don't have enough space where you live you can try a basement at a community center, a park or picnic grounds, a friend's house, a union or veterans' hall, or any public space that's available. (Some public spaces do not permit election-related events, and others prohibit alcohol. Check first before you make plans.)

Create an invitation. A simple e-mail or paper invitation followed by a phone call is sufficient. Provide directions to your party and ask for an RSVP so you can prepare. On your invitation, explain what you have planned. Tell your invitees to bring their friends and, if you plan to ask for money, their checkbook. Suggest ways for your invitees to volunteer, register to vote, request a mail-in ballot, or donate even if they cannot attend. (You can find a sample invitation at showgeorgethedoor.org.)

Have a sign-in sheet to collect names and contact information from all attendees. Use this to recruit volunteers later. Ask people to add their friends to the list.

Make sure everyone leaves the party with something to do. Plan a day for voter registration or any other action from this book.

 for practical, concerned, and busy people.

"Host" a house party that nobody attends. Perfect for the busy person. You tell your friends that it's the first fundraising party that they don't have to attend. No speeches to listen to, no grapes to nibble. No one attends this house party, because you don't really hold one.

Theme: Honorable Discharge Party. Your friends can say they attended if they give a donation or have their dad send in a donation for them.

Refreshments: None

Games: None

 for anti-Bush patriots with time to spare.

Host a house party and make sure one of your friends throws one, too. For theme ideas, see Chapter 8, More House Party Themes.

 for the anybody-but-Bush guerilla.

MEDIA FRIENDLY: Host a "Pin the Lie on Bush" party.

Theme: Bush Lies

Refreshments: Nuts, because Bush is nuts and most guerillas are vegetarian.

Game: Bushocchio or Pin the Lie on Bush. Play this like "Pin the Tail on the Donkey," with a blindfold, a photo of Bush, and a Pinocchio-like nose that contestants try to pin on the presidential face. (Download the nose and face from showgeorgethedoor.org.)

Bushism

"I know how hard it is for you to put food on your family."
—George W. Bush, Greater Nashua, New Hampshire,
January 27, 2000

Resources

For sample party invitations and Bushocchio game, visit showgeorgethedoor.org.

If you plan to raise money at your house party for an organization or a candidate, check with the future recipient of your donations before your house party to make sure you're clear on all the rules that might apply to donations that you collect.

For more tips on house parties and fundraising, see Kim Klein, *Fundraising for Social Change*, John Wiley and Sons, 2000.

To obtain mail-in ballot request forms for your state, visit nasad.org/statelinks.htm and click on your state's Web site.

For voter registration forms visit fec/votregis/vr.htm and click on "For Public Use."

8. *MORE HOUSE PARTY THEMES*

Consider adding a theme to your house party for voting, registering voters, recruiting volunteers, or fundraising, as described in the last chapter, consider having a themed house party on a different date. Themes can make parties more fun. And fun is what gets people involved when they're not motivated by Bush's dismal record alone.

The food and activities at these house parties are limited only by your own imagination and your practical goals. Some of our ideas are described below.

 for practical, concerned, and busy people.

Just make a donation. Hosting a house party takes time, but a donation is always a strong way to contribute if you have no time to spare.

 for anti-Bush patriots with time to spare.

A July 4 "Patriots for Regime Change" party

Theme: It's your patriotic duty to defeat Bush. Amazingly, there are over 150 patriotic July 4 products at bulkpartysupplies.com or use Show George the Door napkins (showgeorgethedoor.com).

Refreshments: Patriotic foods like French fries and apple pie.

Games: Bushocchio (see previous chapter).

Crawford vacation party

Theme: The first night of a month's vacation in Crawford, Texas.

Refreshments: Tex-Mex food, Coors.

Games: Horse shoes, pick the next target for invasion on world map.

Bushism party

Theme: Bush is stranger than fiction.

Refreshments: "Mad cow" hamburgers.

Games: Guests try to identify the actual Bush quotes from a list of real quotes and those you make up. (You can get real Bush quotes from Jacob Weisberg's collection at dubyaspeak.com.)

Energy policy committee party

Theme: You've been named to Dick Cheney's secret group of oil policy executives to formulate energy policy.

Refreshments: Paté, brie, caviar.

Games: Give a prize to the person who comes up with the most ridiculous excuse for: keeping the names of the committee members secret, continuing the current reliance on fossil fuels, or refusing to invest in renewables.

Halloween party

Theme: Pumpkin carving

Refreshments: Candy, hot cider.

Games: Prizes are awarded for the pumpkin that best symbolizes Bush and the most artfully carved slogan (like "Vote Bush Out") from a pumpkin. (Don't wait for Halloween to get these on your porch with candles!)

 for the anybody-but-Bush guerilla.

Bush sign party

Theme: Irreverence

Refreshments: Steamed spinach for healthy and strong guerillas.

Games: Cut up a Bush yard sign into tiny pieces and put them all into a big gallon jar. Partiers guess how many pieces are in the jar. Award a prize to the person who guesses closest to the actual number. (Select your prize from the great Bush gifts described in Chapter 4, Gift for the Election Season) Also, have a few Bush signs and scissors around in case your guests want to cut up their own.

Bushism

"Oftentimes, we live in a processed world—you know, people focus on the process and not results."—George W. Bush, Washington D.C., November 29, 2003

Resources

Source of patriotic party stuff: bulkpartysupplies.com.

Sample party invitations can be found at showgeorgethedoor.org.

For prize ideas, see Chapter 4, Gifts for the Election Season.

9. GIVE MONEY

Bush and Cheney hop around the country hosting $1,000-per-plate fundraising dinners. That often translates into $1 million per hop. There's no way we can match this, even if we hop nonstop between now and Election Day.

That's why taking action is so important. We can get more done than Bush, even if we can't raise more money.

And although we can't match the Bush fundraising machine, our side has to be in the fundraising ballpark—even if it's in the outfield—if we want to have a prayer of winning.

That's why, in addition to volunteering your time, you should consider donating to an organization working on an issue you care about—or you could simply contribute to the Democratic Party.

As you've heard before, any amount helps. You have to imagine millions of others, who might have as little to give as you, donating as well. That's how your money, even if it's minimal, will make a difference.

To make sure you do not break any fundraising laws, figure out which organization want to donate to. Then contact the group to find out what fundraising rules apply to it.

 for practical, concerned, and busy people.

Give whatever you can afford. Giving money is by far the most practical action that the concerned and busy person can take. It can take as little as three minutes.

 for anti-Bush patriots with time to spare.

Write personal letters to a dozen friends. Collect enough money to match half a plate at a George W. Bush fundraiser. That means $500. Check out a sample letter on showgeorgethedoor.org.

To succeed at this, make a quick plan. Figure out who among your friends could give $10, $30, $50, $100, or more. To reach $500, if that's your goal, ask the people on the top of your list first, and work down. Fundraising experts will tell you that people give most readily if they are asked personally by someone they know, and they are asked more than once. Even if people want to give, they often forget. Consider writing your letters on half of a paper plate to emphasize your goal of raising half the ticket price to a typical Bush fundraising dinner.

 for the anybody-but-Bush guerilla.

Some guerillas would rob a bank, but we don't advocate this. Get a hold of some money and make a donation.

Bushism

"First, let me make it very clear, poor people aren't necessarily killers. Just because you happen to be not rich doesn't mean you're willing to kill."
—George W. Bush, Washington, D.C., May 19, 2003

Resources

For a list of organizations to which you could consider making a donation, see Chapter 5, Help Defeat Bush in Swing States (Even if You Don't Live in One) and Chapter 6, Educate People About an Issue You Care About—and Register Them to Vote.

For a sample letter to friends asking for a donation, visit showgeorgethedoor.org.

10. *TAKE ELECTION DAY OFF FROM WORK TO MOBILIZE VOTERS*

We won't win the next election unless we beg, cajole, beseech, and implore our people to vote. And then we have to plead and beg some more, if necessary, and it never hurts to say "please" a few times. Then, we have to offer them a ride to the polls if they need it, maybe watch their kids while they're voting, and do whatever else is legal and proper.

That's what campaign volunteers do on Election Day—on the phone, on foot, in their cars, on their computers. In the months and years leading up the election, campaign workers assemble lists of people who say they will vote for their candidate.

Election Day and the weekend prior to it are by far the most critical days to reach as many of these voters as possible.

One of the most effective ways to do this is still the least high-tech— walk through neighborhoods of likely supporters and urge them to vote. Campaigns will send volunteer "poll watchers" to polling places to find out how many people in the area are voting, and they will call likely voters who haven't shown up. Or they will walk through the neighborhood encouraging people to vote.

You should seriously consider joining this effort.

And to do it best, you should take a vacation day from your job on Election Day. Or take half a day off. Or whatever amount of the day you can afford. Or canvass on the weekend of October 30 and 31.

A few enlightened employers may give you the day off, if you ask for it. Other employers will at least give you time off to vote, giving you more time to beg people to vote once you're away from the job.

Plan for it by asking your boss, if you need to, as soon as possible.

In fact, we all might suggest to our bosses that they give *all employees* an hour off on Election Day to vote.

But if your boss is stingy, apathetic, Bush-loving, greedy, or whatever, take a vacation day for the sake of the planet.

 for practical, concerned, and busy people.

Get a friend to take the day off. There may be serious conflict between "concerned and practical" and busy on Election Day. If you're concerned and practical, you should take Election Day off work. Getting people to vote is about as practical as it gets. But if you're busy, maybe you can't. If that's the case, convince someone else to do it on your behalf. Or, in the time-honored tradition of paying people to fight for you, offer cash to someone to take the day off for you and get out the vote.

Volunteer for a few hours. A few weeks before November 2, call local advocacy groups or your local Democratic Party campaign office, and tell them how much time you've got available and when. (See Resources below.)

 for anti-Bush patriots with time to spare.

Dedicate Election Day or the weekend prior to getting out the vote. Connect with an organization or your local Democratic Party office and put in as many hours as you can.

 for the anybody-but-Bush guerilla.

Go crazy. Many guerillas, who are most comfortable on the edge of society, won't be inspired to join the Democratic Party activities—or any organized activity. We would advise setting these feelings aside for a day, but if you can't, that's okay. Pick one of the more eye-popping actions in this book, like Chapter 15, Dress in Costume; Chapter 3, Pets for Regime Change; or Chapter 14, Find a Street Corner and Wear a Sandwich Board, and execute it all day long on Election Day.

Bushism

"It was amazing I won. I was running against peace and prosperity and incumbency."—George W. Bush, Gothenberg, Sweden, June 14, 2001

Resources

For swing state activities, see Chapter 5, Help Defeat Bush in Swing States (Even if You Don't Live in One).

For groups promoting specific issues, see Chapter 6, Educate People About an Issue You Care About—and Register Them to Vote.

Visit Democrats.org (202-863-8000) for a list of state Democratic Party offices.

★ ON THE STREETS ★

11. ACTIVATING THE BODY POLITIC

Yes, a button is a beautiful thing. With fewer and fewer people wearing them, they are even more powerful today than they used to be. Even simple political buttons (like "Vote!") are great—and we've listed good sources for them below.

But think about wearing something unusual, like a bug, so people will ask about it at the water fountain, and you can draw people into a conversation about how important it is to vote.

"Uh, Ben, what's with the bug button on your shirt?"

"Bush bugs me. I want people to vote against him."

"Jason, what's with the nose clips around your neck?"

"I'm giving them to Republicans so they can hold their nose, if they must, and vote for a Democrat in November."

We need to put our bodies on the line to win this election. Tattoos are great, but if they are not for you, you can put your body on the line without putting lines on your body.

This is no time to hide our anti-Bush sentiments in an undisclosed location. If we all wear our opposition to Bush on our sleeves, and everywhere else, our campaign will have more momentum. So consider doing your part with a body part. It's patriotic.

 *for practical, concerned, and busy people.*

Make a political fashion statement. There are opportunities all over your body. Earrings, armbands, neckties, T-shirts, necklaces, hats, you name it. Pick a body part or two and you're off and running. (For sources of anti-Bush garb, see Resources below.)

for anti-Bush patriots with time to spare.

Dress up your friends. Pick your favorite anti-Bush fashions and take orders from others who want to buy them. You could stroll around the office offering likeminded colleagues samples of what's available.

 for the anybody-but-Bush guerilla.

Guerillas, being small in number but big in resourceful-ness, find every possible way to get others to do their work for them. So, when it comes to "The Body Politic," guerillas pre-fer to use someone else's body.[2] Here's what you do: Buy a bunch of "Show George the Door" stickers and keep them in your pocket every day until November 2. When you cross paths with a diehard Bush supporter, place a sticker—with the sticky side exposed and facing out—in the palm of your hand. Then, with the sticker cupped in your hand, reach around the back of the Bush support-er and slap him or her very gently on the back. (Don't slap too hard; the best guerillas always practice nonviolence.) And watch the Bushie walk away unwittingly doing his or her part to take back our country.

Bushism

"Do you have blacks, too?"—George W. Bush, to Brazilian President Fernando Cardoso, November 8, 2001

Resources

For nose clips: holdyournoseandvote.org, and for "Show George the Door Stickers:" showgeorgethedoor.org.

There is a plethora of buttons out there from *The Nation* magazine's Bush-with-Pinocchio-nose button (thenation.com, click on "shop" then "protest gear") and "He Lied, They Died" pin (thenation.com)

---

[2] Not "use" in the bad sense, of course.

to plain old campaign buttons (kerrygear.com). Here are some samples of the button gambit (from the buttonshack.com and donnelly-colt.com):

☛ The concise and straightforward: "Boot Bush," "Fire Bush," "Bush Sucks," or "Re-Defeat Bush 2004."

☛ The crass: "Bush: 666."

☛ The clever: "Asses of Evil: Bush-Cheney-Ashcroft-Rumsfeld" or "Scrub Shrub 2004."

☛ The conservatively anti-Bush: "Save Democracy: Vote Democrat."

☛ The can't-go-wrong button: "Bush" (circled with a line through it) or "Re-defeat Bush 2004."

For insect pins: insectsinside.com.

Neckties can also make that patriotic statement (ties.com) or proclaim your party affiliation. For some classier looking Democrat ties: tigereyedesign.com.

T-shirts, like buttons, cover the whole range of political boldness. There is something for rabid anti-Bush people who wear their political leanings on their sleeves (literally) to something more subdued. Check out politicalclothing.com or seeyageorge.com. And this is a good outfit: jimmorris.com.

12. YOUR CAR AS A MOVING BILLBOARD

For those of us who own cars, it's time to use them to spread the word.

First, bumper stickers. You may notice that you don't see as many bumper stickers as you used to. Why? Apathy is one reason. But another significant reason is that cars are so beloved that people who own them don't want to blemish their bumpers, even with something as vital as a "Register to Vote" bumper sticker.

If you're overly protective of your bumper and have eschewed sticking anything on it, get over it, please. As the use of bumper stickers has declined, more people read them—because there are fewer out there.

If you don't like bumper stickers, advertise your opposition to Bush with a banner on your car roof. A typical roof rack can hold a three-by-five-foot banner running like a cab advertisement on the roof. Or put a sign or decal in your window. Or how about an "electrostatic" that has no adhesive but still sticks to your window?

The easiest way to procure a window sign for your car is to transform a yard sign. Just pull out the wire spikes that you'd use to place a yard sign in the ground and put the sign itself in your car window.

There's also a three-dimensional Pants-on-Fire window dangler for the rear-view mirror that doesn't block you vision, available at show-georgethedoor.org. (This is your chance to be like the cool guys in high school who had those dice.)

Yet another option for creative folks is to buy window markers and go to town on the side or back windows of your car. You can draw pictures or create simple slogans. (White usually works best on a window.) The paint from this type of marker, which comes in a glue-stick-like container, will withstand quite a bit of weather before disappearing. And you can easily scrape it off if, God forbid, you are given shock treatments, go insane, and decide to switch and vote for Bush.

for practical, concerned, and busy people.

Leave No Billionaire Behind
Billionaires for Bush

Leave no bumper without a bumper sticker.

Credit: Billionaires for Bush is a do-it-yourself street theater and media campaign. Visit billionairesforbush.com to join up and get more stuff.

Put your favorite anti-Bush bumper sticker on your car. It may seem insignificant, but do it anyway. Maybe you don't like bumper stickers on your car. If so, you are perfect for this because you've got a sticker-free bumper, so your anti-Bush sticker will stand out—and dumping Bush is worth a one-month defacement of your pretty bumper, right? If you can't bring yourself to do this, you might try a window decal. And get some for your friends.

 for anti-Bush patriots with time to spare.

Buy bumper stickers, window decals, electrostatic clings, suction danglers, window paint, and window signs for yourself and a dozen friends. Select your favorite bumper

sticker and car-window poster (the poster part of a typical yard sign) and buy twelve of each. Then make sure that each of the twelve people you give these to actually puts them on their cars. Also, buy twelve paint sticks (like glue sticks) of white window paint and pass them out to twelve different people, with a plea to write something like "Vote Bush Out" on the back windows of at least twelve of their friends' cars. (See Resources below.)

"Liar, Liar, Pants on Fire" window decal.

Credit: pantsonfire.net

for the anybody-but-Bush guerilla.

Act from a moving car. Blast a taped announcement from your car on Election Day, reminding people to vote. Drive in areas where most voters would be with us. Or try this, even if it's less strategic, which is okay because guerillas aren't always strategic. (That's why wonks often despise them.) Guerillas sometimes love to tease and needle, even if it accomplishes nothing tangible. In his book *Had Enough? A Handbook for Fighting Back*, James Carville suggests that, when you see a Bush bumper sticker, pull up alongside the driver, roll down your window, and shout, "Hey, someone put a Bush bumper sticker on your car." Then, give them a blast of an anti-Bush song from your car stereo. (See Chapter 24, Songs in the Key of Regime Change, for available CDs.)

Bushism

"We need an energy bill that encourages consumption."
—George W. Bush, Trenton, New Jersey, September 23, 2002

Resources

Get your "Leave No Billionaire Behind" bumper sticker at BillionairesforBush.com. Other gems on the site are: "Blood for Oil," "Free the Enron 7," and "Corporations are People Too." Another favorite of ours is "Save the Environment: Plant a Bush Back in Texas." (Seeyageorge.com.)

Can't find a bumper sticker that perfectly makes your point? Get some custom stickers printed at StickerNation.com.

Don't want to peel off that bumper sticker after the election? Print your own electrostatic decals, which stick to your window without adhesive, at ultimatedecals.com. It has a gallery of artwork you can customize. We like the Uncle Sam, which has a space for you to write your own comment like, "Better off WITHOUT you, George."

Maybe you want to make your own message and dangle it from your window. If so, here's a place to get suction cups with clips or hooks: suctioncupsinc.com.

You can download flyers from WhoDies.com (We especially appreciate the flyer that reads: "After the war, Dick Cheney will have a job. Will you?")

Pick up a campaign yard sign from your local Democratic Party office (democrats.org) and put it in your car window.

Tell your neighbors where you stand with a "Regime Change Begins at Home: VOTE OUT Bush/Cheney" yard sign or flyer from the Syracuse Cultural Workers (syrculturalworkers.com).

Call your local art supply store for window paint. You can get the glue-stick-like variety or tubs.

Get a "Pants on Fire" decal and window dangler at showgeorgethe-door.org, which also offers these stickers: "Show George the Door, Vote 2004," "Anybody But Bush," "Broke at Home, Hated Abroad," (with a photo of Bush with a red line across him), "04" (with a photo of Bush in the "0" with a red line across him).

13. *YOUR HOUSE VERSUS THE WHITE HOUSE*

There's a reason you see all the signs for candidates in your neighborhood during election season: They actually work.

Lots and lots of folks are confused about whom to vote for—or whether to vote at all. And many people trust their neighbors, even if they don't know them. Your neighbors might remember that they saw a candidate's sign in your yard or apartment window and this might make a difference when they push, punch or do whatever they do in the ballot booth.

Like any other visible support for a candidate, yard signs help boost the momentum of a campaign, which fires up volunteers and staff—and energizes fundraising efforts.

So, yard signs are good.

But you can do more with your domicile than throw up a yard sign. And have more fun. And get more attention.[3]

 for the practical, concerned, and busy person.

Call the campaign and order a yard sign. Simply call the office of the Democratic Party in your state (Democrats.org or 202-863-8000). They will most likely deliver a sign to your door.

 for anti-Bush patriots with time to spare.

For the energetic, the possibilities are vast, using as much red, white, and blue as possible:

° Hang a banner from your porch or second-story window (Dump Bush. Vote.).

° Spell "Vote Bush Out" with Christmas lights.

---

3 Some cities have rules regulating the placement, size, location, number, and duration of political signs on property, homes, and elsewhere. If you're planning something major, a quick call to the city clerk could help you avoid receiving a threatening note. Another approach is to take down what you put up, if and when the authorities ask you to do so. Temporary signs, banners, and signs on wheels are less likely to be regulated.

° Paint a message on your roof.

° Put a sign in your window.

 for the anybody-but-Bush guerilla.

Build banners for others. Some guerillas, being anything but passive, un-decorate the lawn signs on the houses of the Bushies. But we do not advocate this. Instead, we suggest that guerillas think big, as guerillas are wont to do, and construct one of those huge political signs that you often see along highways and in vacant lots. To do this, you'll have to put your innate industriousness to work: You'll need to make the sign yourself—or with the help of your comrades—out of sturdy materials. And you will have to find a good capitalist willing to let you use his or her land. Try ranchers or farmers. The owners of all property are part of the public record. Target an area, and have at it.

Bushism

"It is white."—George W. Bush, when asked by a child in Britain what the White House was like, July 19, 2001

Resources

When it comes to window paint, you have a couple of options: glass markers, which work like glue sticks, and actual paint for windows. The latter comes in a tub like regular paint and is a bit more expensive. Call your local art supply store to see what they carry.

Your state Democratic Party office (democrats.org) should have a yard sign for you, or you can order a "Regime Change Begins at Home" sign from the Syracuse Cultural Workers (syrculturalworkers.com).

For window decorations see the Resources section of the previous chapter.

14. FIND A STREET CORNER AND
WEAR A SANDWICH BOARD

If you live in an urban, or even a semi-urban area, there's a good chance you see panhandlers on your morning commute. As a matter of fact, with millions losing their jobs during the Bush presidency, you probably see more panhandlers than you did four years ago.

Even if you never give a dime to anyone on the street, you have to notice them. They're out during rush hour. They're human beings standing or pacing along busy streets.

These people could use some help—and some company. And you can do both, in the name of regime change.

 for practical, concerned, and busy people.

This action is not for those of you who self-identify with "practical." Skip this and find another action in this book that's better suited to your temperament and schedule.

 for anti-Bush patriots with time to spare.

Give T-shirts to panhandlers on street corners. A shirt with the message "Better off than you were four years ago? Me neither" works well (get it printed by zazzle.com or make some of your own with fabric paint on a solid-color T-shirt), but give away whatever regime-change articles of clothing you can find. People will notice and, hopefully, give more money to your new friend. (You can give money, too.)

 for the anybody-but-Bush guerilla.

MEDIA FRIENDLY: Be a human billboard. Guerillas are used to street life. Make a sign and find a busy street corner. For a sign, try: BETTER OFF THAN YOU WERE FOUR YEARS AGO? ME NEITHER. And think big. Create one of those sandwich boards, which consist of two body-sized pieces of wood or cardboard attached by two pieces of rope. The rope fits over your shoulders, holding one sign on your front and one on your back, with you in the middle as the "filling" for the "sandwich."

P.S. If you join panhandlers on the street, give them a generous, liberal handout.

We'll all be better off if we vote Bush out in November.

Credit: Jesse Mangerson

Bushism

"I need to be able to move the right people to the right place at the right time to protect you, and I'm not going to accept a lousy bill out of the United Nations Senate."
—George W. Bush, South Bend, Indiana, October 31, 2002

Resources

Custom T-shirts: zazzle.com seems to have a fast turnaround. You can use your own creative graphics or borrow ours in the "contributors" section of zazzle.com.

15. DRESS IN A COSTUME

Election campaigns these days are mostly theater, with candidates dashing from stage to stage in different cities, brandishing different props at each stop. So, in an age of theatrical politics, it's not at all surprising that costumes are a great tool to get attention.

Recall, for example, that one of the lasting images of President Clinton's campaign against Senator Bob Dole in 1996 was the "Buttman," which was a Democratic Party activist dressed in a cigarette-butt costume. Buttman dogged Dole around the country, linking him to the powerful and evil tobacco lobby.

In another campaign, one of the candidates resisted debating his opponent (kinda like our current president). In response, the opponent's supporters sent a "duck" to rallies to heckle the candidate who refused to debate. A survey of local media coverage of this election revealed that the duck waddled away with more airtime than most of the substantive issues in the election. The candidate supported by the duck won hands down.

The Working Families Party in New York got an ostrich costume to illustrate its point that Hillary Rodham Clinton's opponent, Rick Lazio, had his "head in the sand" on economic issues, much to the pleasure of the news media.

Even if your costume doesn't make the news, it will turn a lot of heads. Think of all the costumed mascots that grab people's attention along the highway, like the human-sized taco, dripping with rubber-ized lettuce and cheese, that was dancing by the taco stand the other day. You didn't see it? Thousands of other people did. They were honking their horns at it and waving, and they probably will go back for a taco some time.

You don't have to own a taco corporation to employ the same PR tactics.

Think of all the costumes that could be used against George Bush. Here are a few ideas, coupled with suggested signs that you could carry if you dress up.

Costume	Sign that You Carry
Skunk	You Stink if You Don't Vote
Duck	Bush is Ducking the Debates
Chicken	Bush is Too Chicken to Debate
Ostrich	Bush's Head is in the Sand About the Economy
Santa Claus	Bush is Santa Claus for the Wealthy
Bunny	Lettuce Vote Bush Out
Frog	Bush is Slimier than I Am
Turkey	You're a Turkey if You Don't Vote

 for practical, concerned, and busy people.

Propose to a friend that you'll pay for the rental of the duck costume if he or she wears it and makes a sign (like "Bush Is Ducking the Debates"). Dressing in costume is a lot to ask of a practical, busy person, even though it might be more fun than you think. But you can certainly propose the idea to a friend.

 for anti-Bush patriots with time to spare.

MEDIA FRIENDLY: Dress in a costume and stand on a street corner. Get together with at least three friends, don your costumes and signs, and entertain all who pass you. Or take shifts in one costume.

for the anybody-but-Bush guerilla.

The true guerilla is relentless and therefore knows that pestering Bush in one city alone isn't enough. So, think bigger. Find fellow guerillas in five states. As a group, agree on one costume that you will each wear the day before Bush arrives in your town and in front of—or as close as you can get to—the actual Bush event.

Bushism

"You've also got to measure in order to begin to effect change that's just more—when there's more than talk, there's just actual—a paradigm shift."—George W. Bush, Washington, D.C., July 1, 2003

Resources

Costumes don't have to be expensive to be effective. Check out the $8 masks or face painting supplies at allcostumes.com. Costumeman.com has a smorgasbord of full-body costumes for under $30. Just add imagination. Get old standby Uncle Sam at buycostumes.com.

Most large cities have costume shops, and costumes rent from $50 or more per day. Just look in the yellow pages under "costume."

Many costume shops are owned by artsy people who'd love to extract Bush from the White House. So, if you're short on cash, call a few costume shops in your area, tell them what you want to do, and see if you can get a costume free or discounted for a day or two.

16. *WHEN BUSH AND COMPANY VISIT, PROTEST!*

Why, you might reasonably wonder, should I bother protesting when Bush comes to my town? No one can get near him anyway, and presidential protests seem ineffective and tiresome, with demonstrators waiting around as the President's arrival is delayed and delayed again. And when he does show up, the Prez is whisked in and out of a photo op, and you've lost three hours that you could have spent trying to convince your Republican mother-in-law to walk her talk about the environment and vote Democrat.

Yes, it seems like a waste of time, but protesting Bush, Cheney, and their ilk when they swing through your city is actually one of the top ways you can help show George the door.

The reason? The media.

When Bush comes to town, it's a guaranteed media event, not only for local media, but often for a chunk of the national news media as well—which, of course, reaches into swing states.

Even if every local protest doesn't make national news, it will still be covered in your community, and the pack of national reporters who

Hit the streets when Bush and Company visit.   *Credit: Jesse Mangerson*

travel with Bush will take note of the level of opposition dogging the candidate. Reporters' impressions of the intensity, size, and diversity of the demonstrators will seep into their stories.

So, if those of us who want to defeat Bush can string together large and emotionally charged demonstrations at stop after stop on the campaign trail, the story of sustained opposition—along with powerful images of dissent—will be told nationally.

 for practical, concerned, and busy people.

When Bush or his surrogates comes to town, don't make up any excuses. Give it your best effort to go to the rally!

 for anti-Bush patriots with time to spare.

Call five people the night before the demonstration and convince them to attend the anti-Bush rally. Calling on the phone is much more effective than sending an e-mail. Try to get them to actually say they will attend: "So, Charlie, will I see you at the rally?" If Charlie says yes, there's a much better chance he will actually be there.

 for the anybody-but-Bush guerilla.

While passive people whisper, guerillas love to chant and make loud and productive noise. And they like to do it in groups. So, when you go to the anti-Bush rally, find ten comrades to go with you and get the crowd chanting. Here are some possibilities:

* Hey, hey, ho, ho, the lying liar has got to go.

* Oh, oh, my, my, Bush and Cheney lie, lie, lie.

* Yo yo, he's got to go. Byyyyyye Bush.

* Bush is a liar. His pants are on fire. End the quagmire.

Bushism

"I've seen all kinds of protests since I've been the President. I remember the protests against trade. A lot of people didn't feel like free trade was good for the world. I completely disagree. I think free trade is good for both wealthy and impoverished nations. But that didn't change my opinion about trade. As a matter of fact, I went to the Congress to get trade promotion authority out."
—George W. Bush, Washington, D.C., March 6, 2003

Resources

Organizations that may protest Bush in your area are: the American Friends Service Committee (afsc.org), Women's International League for Peace and Freedom (wilpf.org), and Raging Grannies (raginggrannies.com).

There are a few books and Web sites that will give you some ideas or spawn some fresh creativity. Check out *Adbusters* magazine (adbusters.org) and the Ruckus Society (ruckus.org) online for info on creative dissent. Also try causecommunications.com.

You can also try *The Activist Cookbook* written by Andrew Boyd (unitedforafaireconomy.org), *Handbook for Nonviolent Action from the War Resisters League* (warresisters.org), or *Pranks* (search researchpubs.com). These books have ideas and step-by-step instructions for protest actions.

For making puppets for protests, check out *68 Ways to Make Really Big Puppets* by Sarah Peatie, Bread and Puppet Press, or *Wise Fool Basics* at zeitgeist.net/wfca/wisefool.htm.

17. RALLY FOR THE DEMOCRAT

The flip side of protesting Bush is supporting the Democrat when he visits your area. This is just as important as protesting Bush.

If the national media see that Bush is greeted with vocal protests and the Democrat with waves of cheers, this will be reflected in the news and it will make a difference in every aspect of the Democratic campaign—fundraising, volunteer recruitment, staff morale, everything.

Momentum is a real factor in election campaigns. Audibly and visibly supporting the Democrat is a simple and important action that we should all consider taking.

 for practical, concerned, and busy people.

When the Democrat comes to your town, go to the event and support him. Give it your best effort to go to the rally. And e-mail all your friends about it.

 for anti-Bush patriots with time to spare.

Get at least ten people to attend the rally with you. E-mail whomever might come and make phone calls until you get ten people to commit to attend. Go together, if you can, so no one forgets about it. Going to a rally is more fun with friends anyway.

 for the anybody-but-Bush guerilla.

Develop an e-alert list. Guerillas have high-tech connections. So, they might consider finding someone who could develop an online system for people to be notified quickly by e-mail when the Democratic candidate is coming—or if any event is on the horizon requiring action. Techies can develop simple Listservs that allow people to register with their name, e-mail address, and ZIP code. Or use Yahoo! to do this.

Bushism

"I was proud the other day when both Republicans and Democrats stood with me in the Rose Garden to announce their support for a clear statement of purpose, 'You disarm, or we will.'"—George W. Bush, Manchester, New Hampshire, October 5, 2002

Resources

TrueMajorityACTION. org plans to let its members know when Bush and company are coming to their areas.

18. *CONVENE WITH THE REPUBLICANS*

Even though they're bores, the Democratic and Republican conventions are major media events for both parties. Knowing this, the Republicans are planning their convention in New York from August 30 to Sept. 2, just prior to Sept. 11 commemorations.

By holding their convention in New York a month later than they held it in 2000—and a month after the Democrats hold theirs—the Republicans hope to score back-to-back PR home runs, first with their convention and then with a high-profile commemoration of 9/11.

It won't be the first time Bush and his advisors will build a PR campaign around a 9/11 anniversary. The administration used the anniversary in 2002 to launch its marketing campaign for the Iraq war. Bush and company did not want to start promoting the war in the summer, according to his Chief of Staff Andrew Card, because "from a marketing point of view, you don't introduce new products in August."

And Card knew that Bush's Sept. 11 speech would provide irresistible images for the news media, which it did. Bush dialed up the war rhetoric with the Statue of Liberty in the background, perfectly aglow thanks to three barges with floodlights floating in New York Harbor. The Bush PR machine selected Ellis Island—rather than other locations in New York—for the speech, so the media would have access to dramatic shots of the President and the lighted Statue of Liberty.

The Republicans' crass PR plan for their convention could easily blow up in their faces if enough people get angry about it. Some relatives of people killed in the 9/11 tragedy are considering staging their own demonstration or joining planned protests.

Large, peaceful protests at the Republican Convention would help blunt the Republicans' PR offensive in early September.

for practical, concerned, and busy people.

Call or e-mail anyone you know in New York and urge them to demonstrate on Aug. 29, the day before the Republican National Convention. See Resources below.

 for anti-Bush patriots with time to spare.

If you live on the East Coast and have time to travel to New York, go there for a demonstration. If you've never made a road trip for a protest, you'll enjoy doing it. It's great to step off the car or the bus and join a sea of inspired people.

 for the anybody-but-Bush guerilla.

Go to New York to protest, wherever you live. Guerillas are always looking for a good road trip. This would be a memorable one, especially if you dress in costume as explained in Chapter 15, Dress in a Costume.

Bushism

"Our nation must come together to unite."
—George W. Bush, Tampa, Florida, June 4, 2001

Resources

United for Peace and Justice (unitedforpeace.org) is planning a demonstration and has applied for a permit to hold a rally in Central Park on Sunday, Aug. 29.

More convention-related activities can be found on counterconvention.org and rncnotwelcome.org. Sign up with these groups to receive news and action alerts related to the Republican Convention.

19. CHALKING SIDEWALKS FOR THE GOOD OF THE NATION

In the last few years, the quality of sidewalk chalk has improved expo-
nentially. Now you can get kid-sized buckets of thick chalk in a range
of bright colors, perfect for elementary schoolers who want to draw
pictures on the front porch or squares for hopscotch on the play-
ground.

And the good part is, most kids use only a fraction of the over-sized
chalk packages, leaving plenty for you to utilize for the good of the
nation.

So, borrow some chalk from a young friend or procure some from a
toy store and get to work. Here's how:

☛ Choose a target. Find a sidewalk that will be used by people
   whom you want to see your chalk work.

☛ Select a short phrase that will appeal to your audience. Options
   include: "Vote," "Vote Bush Out," and "No More Bush."

☛ Replicate your phrase. You'll have the most impact if you chalk
   the same phrase repeatedly in a small area where people will see
   it more than once.

☛ Work at off hours. Your sidewalk decorating should be done
   when the crowds are gone.

☛ Respect local customs. If this benign activity is banned in your
   area, don't do it. And if people get angry and demand that you
   clean it up, do so. Apologize and move on.

 for practical, concerned, and busy people.

Skip this. It doesn't pass the practicality test.

for anti-Bush patriots with time to spare.

Write "Vote Bush Out" on the sidewalks in front of ten coffee shops. Young adults, widely viewed as key to defeating George, are big-time coffee shop attendees. This is a way to speak to them.

 for the anybody-but-Bush guerilla.

Make a chalk stamper, and hit the sidewalks. Guerillas strive for maximum efficiency with minimum effort. So, when it comes to sidewalk chalking, true guerillas use a chalk stamp pad. This is like a big version of a rubber stamp that you might use in an office. Here's how you create one and use it boot Bush.

1. Find a couple of friends, because it's more fun to do this with company. It's a bonding experience.

2. Get the stuff on the shopping list below. (Try a locally owned hardware store or, if you must, all items are available at Home Depot.)

   ° Plywood (five-eighth-inch minimum thickness and about eighteen inches long by about nine inches wide).

   ° At least four nine-inch flat painting pads, called "Pad Painter Refill Pads." We've used a brand called "Shurline." (These will function like the rubber part of an office stamp.)

   ° A pipe flange with threads compatible with the pipe below.

   ° An approximately one-inch-diameter broomstick-like pipe (about four to five feet high) with threads to fit in the flange.

   ° A low plastic basin with a bottom dimension of at least ten by nineteen inches. (So the plywood board will fit in it.)

   ° A half-gallon container of powdered chalk, used for making chalk lines in carpentry. (If you can't find half gallons, buy a bunch of the smaller containers.)

   ° Roundhead (three-quarter-inch long) wood screws to fasten the painting pads to the plywood.

   ° Bolts to attach the flange to the plywood.

° Twelve to sixteen feet of approximately quarter-inch-diameter rope or chain (to make it easy to carry the basin when it's loaded with chalk slurry).

3. Bolt the flange to the middle of the plywood. Start with the bolt head going through the plywood so the nut is on top of the metal flange.

4. We suggest you construct a stamp that says something simple like "Vote Bush Out," with "Vote" on one line and "Bush Out" below it on a separate line.

5. Cut three-and-a-half-inch-high letters out of paper, and flip the paper over so it's backwards and trace around the backwards letters on the pad. (You need the mirror image on the stamp, so the correct image appears where you stamp.)

6. Using a mat knife, cut off the angled tabs along both sides of the pads so the pads will lie flat on the plywood. Cut your letters out of the flat painting pad. DO NOT CUT THROUGH THE PLASTIC BACKING. You can get three to four letters from each pad.

7. Peel the excess pad and foam off the pads. (Now you should have the shapes of letters cut into the pads.)

8. Arrange the pads on the plywood and trim them, if necessary, to get appropriate spacing between letters and words. You may also need to cut out the plastic backing around the bolt heads (holding the plywood to the flange) to allow the pads to lay flat against the plywood.

9. Attach the pads with screws to the plywood starting from the pad side, screwing first through the pad and then into the plywood.

10. Thread the pipe into the flange to create the broomstick-like handle, so you can do your stamping easily while standing up instead of crawling on your hands and knees.

11. Pour some powdered chalk into the basin, add some water, and stir just like you're making polenta. Adjust the proportion of water to chalk powder based on the porosity of the sidewalk you'll be decorating. A little trial and error here is advisable.

12. To make the dipping basin easier to carry, drill or cut three or four holes equally spaced near the top of the sides, and attach the rope or chain.

13. Go to your target location, like the sidewalks in front of coffee shops, and begin. One person stamps and the other carries the basin.

14. You can get many impressions out of one dip. So it's dip, stamp, stamp, stamp, dip, stamp, stamp, stamp, and so on. After dipping, on the first several stamps, stamp lightly, so as not to smudge. As the stamper dries out, you can stamp harder.

This stamp can be used over and over again. When you're done with it, send it to your friends living elsewhere. It's kind of like a chain stamp letter.

For those who are mechanically inclined, you could rig this up as a rotary stamp, like an oversized paint roller.

A chalk stamper makes chalking sidewalks easy.   *Credit: Jesse Mangerson*

Bushism

"It's time to set aside the old partisan bickering and finger-pointing and name-calling that comes from freeing parents to make different choices for their children."
—George W. Bush, Washington, D.C., April 12, 2001

Resources

Any local toy store has buckets of chalk just waiting to make their mark in 2004.

20. *POSTERS PROMOTING A NEW PRESIDENT*

Political activists rely on scrappy PR tactics to get attention: dropping banners from buildings, pasting stickers in phone booths, distributing custom toilet paper, getting arrested, creating puppets for protests, you name it. The best activists—who are at once aggressive and gentle—place a premium on humor and creativity, while staying "on message."

One of the oldest and most venerable ways to raise the profile of an issue or political candidate is to use street posters. Posters may seem insignificant compared to television and the Internet, but we can't afford to overlook anything in the campaign for a new President, and besides, people read 'em. (Why else would the film industry spend millions papering the U.S. with movie posters?)

Posters are especially useful because you can put them up precisely where your "target audience" will see them. For example, if you are targeting younger voters, think about coffee shops or universities.

 for practical, concerned, and busy people.

Hire a student to poster a campus. Select a downloadable poster from the Resources below and pay someone to download it, make copies, and blanket your nearest university campus with them. Do you know a high school or college student, babysitter, or a twenty-something who's angry at Bush? There's someone out there waiting for you to ask.

 for anti-Bush patriots with time to spare.

Put one hundred posters up in your town. Choose a poster, copy one hundred of them, and get to work yourself. Focus on campuses, coffee shops, senior centers, parks, markets, soccer fields—or anywhere you can legally hang a poster. Tape works well, but it's better to use a staple gun.

for the anybody-but-Bush guerilla.

Plaster your city with street posters. While your average person looks at a dark street and sees only bus shelters, lampposts, Dumpsters, and deserted buildings, an anybody-but-Bush guerilla sees fertile ground for "wheatpasting"—one of the finest arts of political expression, using glue made of wheat flour to affix posters to large objects. It's up to you to find legal places to do this. Check the laws, customs, and mores in your community.

Bushism

"If I answer questions every time you ask one,
expectations would be high. And as you know,
I like to keep expectations low."
—George W. Bush, Washington, D.C., December 10, 2002

Resources

Adbusters magazine (adbusters.org) has good tips for postering, as does the "guerilla postering" section of Robbie Conal's Web site (robbieconal.com) and the "guerilla toolbox" section of causecommunications.com.

Staple gun: we recommend seeking out a locally owned hardware or craft store to buy this item.

Progressiveaustin.org has a bunch of graphics, both flyers and posters, that you can print out and use.

Stopbush.com has a wide collection of downloadable posters and flyers.

21. BANNERS AGAINST BUSH

Some activists spotlight an issue by climbing buildings, trees, or other tall objects, and dangling a giant banner down, to the amazement of onlookers. Greenpeace is the master of this, having orchestrated "banner drops" from the Sears Tower, the Statue of Liberty, the Golden Gate Bridge, Congressional office buildings, and other incredibly frightening places from which to be hanging from a rope and holding a banner.

You don't have to be this brave—or crazy—to put banners to work for a cause like regime change at home. The AIDS quilt, for example, was simply a patchwork of cloth made by people in the memory of AIDS victims. Nothing too fancy, but it turned into one of the most memorable and beautiful symbols of the fight against AIDS.

At the local level, banners have been pieced together using people's photos, copies of the covers of banned books, thousands of signatures, and much more. Businesses have erected large banners on their property with political messages.

Here are a few suggestions on how you can put banners to use in your effort to get a new President.

 for practical, concerned, and busy people.

Pay for a plane to carry a sign like "Dump Bush. Vote." If you've ever spent a day on the beach in the summer, you've probably seen planes towing banners like "All You Can Eat Crabs at Dingo's." Many cities, particularly along the coasts, have businesses that will fly your banner from a plane for a day, an hour, or whatever you can afford. All it takes is a phone call and a credit card. (If you do this, work with an anti-Bush organization that will make sure you don't run afoul of campaign expenditure rules.)

A good banner sums it all up in a simple phrase.   *Credit: Jesse Mangerson*

 for anti-Bush patriots with time to spare.

MEDIA FRIENDLY: Create a quilt-type banner highlighting a local problem caused by Bush. For example, you might try to make a giant quilt with squares representing people who have lost their jobs during the last four years in your area, and display it outdoors during the summer. (Alternatively, you could create a large pile of old shoes of the unemployed who've worn out their soles looking for work.)

 for the anybody-but-Bush guerilla.

Take action when the "guerilla moment" presents itself. The tactics of the nonviolent guerilla have been circumscribed somewhat in the post-9/11 world. Climbing bridges and buildings—and dangling banners from them—isn't as easy as it used to be, and carries added risks. So, when it comes to unveiling banners, guerillas have been forced to wait for the right "guerilla moment" rather than on the spectacular banner drop. This means the anybody-but-Bush guerilla has to come up with a great slogan and display it—strung across two hand-held posts—at exactly the right place and time. Usually, the right time is in the middle of a media frenzy, when reporters are looking for something visual to accompany a story that's in the news. Guerillas "hook" their message to an event that's already being covered.

Here's an example of how it's done: "A plucky 61-year-old grand-mother perched atop the gates of the heavily-guarded Buckingham Palace and raising an anti-Bush banner was set to become the enduring image of the nationwide fury over U.S. President George W. Bush's four-day visit to Britain." The banner said, "Elizabeth Windsor and Co. He's not welcome."

And this comes from the *The Hindu* (November 19, 2003), a news-paper out of India, so you know banners are good for some far-flung media attention.

Bushism

"This foreign policy stuff is a little frustrating."—George W. Bush, in the *New York Daily News*, April 23, 2002

Resources

For more information about the AIDS quilt, visit aidsquilt.org.

Look under Signs or Banners in your local phone directory for pro-fessionals who create signs and banners or make your own. Internet-based companies also do this.

22. WALKING DOOR-TO-DOOR

Research shows that the most effective way to motivate people to vote is to talk to them, face to face. Yes, political advertising, phone banking, yard signs, and dressing up like the devil all get attention and can make a difference, but face-to-face contact is number one.

And the most useful (as in strategic) way to do this is also extremely distasteful for many would-be activists: walking door-to-door.

But once you get started, it turns out that ringing doorbells and talking to people is the single most gratifying activity in a political campaign. There's no better way to appreciate and understand people—in all their complexity—than to visit the places where they live.

Which is not to say walking door-to-door is easy or necessarily pretty. There are some rude, angry, and apathetic people out there, many of whom have very frightening dogs in their homes.

But there are many more nice people with dogs so well trained and coiffed that you'll feel guilty about your own wild mutt. So, as you walk door-to-door, keep your eye on the big picture and appreciate the diversity of our own species, as well as that of the canine life form.

And don't worry about being an expert on the issues. *Canvassing is less about convincing folks to vote against Bush and more about increasing voter turnout among those who are already inclined to vote against him—a necessity if we are to win in November.* This doesn't mean you should be ignorant about Bush's record, but you don't need to be a walking wonk. If you don't know an answer to a question, you can always refer people elsewhere. Your primary goal is to inspire people who already lean against Bush to vote.

Here's how you do it:

Join a group. This is important. Rather than walk door-to-door on your own, it's best to join with an organization that has a canvass operation in place. It will have lists and a strategic plan. If there's a particular issue you feel strongly about—and Bush has given us plenty to choose from—find a nonpartisan group that's educating voters on it. (See Chapter 6, Educate People About an Issue You Care About—and Register Them to Vote and Chapter 5, Help Defeat Bush in Swing States (Even if You Don't Live in One). Or link up with your local Democratic Party office (democrats.org or 202-863-8000).

Practice. Any canvassing group that you volunteer to work with will train you prior to putting you on the street. A coach will pretend to be a potential voter and you will pretend to be a canvasser—and you will go through the drill. Most likely, your training will include pointers like the ones below.

Look conventional. There's no point in alienating anyone by your clothes. So err on the side of conventional. If you have a choice, select an area where you'll talk to people like yourself, allowing you to be most persuasive. For example, a study cited by the Campaign for Young Voters shows that if young adults are canvassed by their peers, as opposed to middle-aged types like us, voter turnout increases by 8 percent, enough to have changed the outcome in various races last time.

Evenings and weekends. You want to canvass when most people are home, which means after work and on weekends. Don't knock on doors past 9 p.m., come back to a house that you visit during dinner, and don't start before 9 a.m. on Saturday and Sunday.

Rain is good. Don't skip bad weather. People are impressed—and inspired—if you are out in the cold or dripping wet.

Work in pairs. Canvassing has risks that you will have to assess. It's always safer to walk in pairs, with one of you on each side of the street. It's also more fun this way.

Ring the doorbell. Don't be like Charlie Brown who won't ring the doorbell when he's finally found the nerve to visit the house of the red-headed girl—and so she never comes to the door and he happily leaves. Seriously, the first house is the hardest. Just ring the bell and get it over with.

Start by saying, "I am not selling anything today."

No lies. No guessing. If you're asked a question and you're not sure of the answer, don't guess. Just write down the questioner's contact information, and tell him or her that someone will call with the answer. Either you or someone from the group you are working with can call back. (See Chapter 27, How to Talk to Bush Supporters, and Part 4, Factual Ammunition: A Bite-Sized Summary of the Bush Record.)

Take notes and recruit more volunteers! You will probably be given a map and list for note taking. Be sure to fill it out carefully, noting whom you've convinced to volunteer and who will put up a yard sign or a bumper sticker. Don't forget to bring a pen.

Use your handouts. Leave them even if folks are not home. You will be given pieces that attach to doorknobs or are placed inside the screen door. Don't litter, and remember that it's illegal to put campaign literature in mailboxes. Write a personal note, when people are out. Give away stickers.

Some folks love to chat, but you have a regime to change. So, respectfully decline invitations for coffee—and try to move on within five minutes.

 for practical, concerned, and busy people.

Try to do this, if you can. Canvassing is really important, but it's time-consuming. Try to make time to do it the weekend before the election and on Election Day.

 for anti-Bush patriots with time to spare.

Canvass for a total of eight hours, and find two friends to join you. Call one of the advocacy groups listed in Chapter 6, Educate People About an Issue You Care About—and Register Them to Vote or your local Democratic Party office (democrats.org). Find out when they need people to walk door-to-door and recruit at least two friends to join you. Knock off your eight hours on one weekend day, or break it up into a few evening sessions.

 fon the anybody-but-Bush guenilla.

Don't walk, run. Guerillas are efficient and tough, and they make it a priority to stay in top physical condition. So, guerillas don't walk door-to-door. They run.

Bushism

"I try to go for longer runs, but it's tough around here at the White House on the outdoor track. It's sad that I can't run longer. It's one of the saddest things about the presidency."
—George W. Bush, August 21, 2002

Resources

Organizations running canvass campaigns: See Chapter 6, Educate People About an Issue You Care About—and Register Them to Vote and Chapter 5, Help Defeat Bush in Swing States (Even if You Don't Live in One).

Democratic Party state offices: democrats.org/states/ or call 202-863-8000.

See Catherine Shaw, *The Campaign Manager*, Westview Press, for good tips on canvassing and other campaign activities.

Your Vote Your Choice, available from the National Association of Independent Colleges and Universities (naicu.edu), explains how to organize nonpartisan voter involvement projects.

For "Show George the Door, Vote 2004" stickers to hand out, visit showgeorgethedoor.org.

See Chapter 1, Register People (Including Yourself) to Vote, and Chapter 2, Vote by Mail-in Ballot.

23. A DOG OR CAR WASH FOR
A CLEANER WHITE HOUSE

If you own a dog, and you receive a flyer like this from a friend or neighbor, how could you not attend?

"Does your dog smell like a weapon of mass destruction? Are your pup's paws as dirty as Rummy's hands? Lack the connections to get Halliburton to clean your pooch? Then come to Jaci's Dog Wash, Saturday, Aug. 5, from noon to 3 p.m. at the corner of Main Street and Union.

"The cost is a minimum of $5 per dog, with all money collected to be donated to defeat George Bush."

Even if they don't quite smell like weapons of mass destruction, most dogs are always in need of a wash. And besides, it's your chance to get to know the neighborhood fauna a bit better.

If dogs aren't your thing, there are always cars. There's a reason why car washes are one of the most popular fundraisers: They work. Most people have a car. And even if it's not that dirty, a car can always be cleaned.

So, check out our suggestions below, decide if you want to clean dogs, cars, or something else, and break out the brushes.

Does your dog smell like a weapon of mass destruction?

Credit: Jesse Mangerson

for practical, concerned, and busy people.

If you happen to see an anti-Bush car or dog wash, stop by.

 for anti-Bush patriots with time to spare.

MEDIA FRIENDLY: Hold a car or dog wash and offer people bumper stickers for their clean bumpers. There's no better place to stick a bumper sticker than a freshly cleaned bumper. So here's the scene: One of you is out on the sidewalk in an ostrich costume, carrying two signs. One reads, "Bush's Head is in the Sand on the Economy." The other reads, "Car Wash for Regime Change at Home." This person is waving at drivers to stop. Meanwhile, the rest of you are washing the cars and offering free bumper stickers for the finished cars of those people who want them. You've got a table with voter registration materials, bumper stickers, and other information.

 for the anybody-but-Bush guerilla.

Go door-to-door for dogs or cars. Since passivity gets you nowhere in the guerilla book of etiquette, pick up your bucket, soap, brushes, vacuum, and rags—along with your register-to-vote and mail-in ballot request forms—and start going door-to-door. You'll be surprised at how many people seem like they are waiting for you to ring their doorbell and ask if they want their car or dog washed. You can make $100 quickly, if you pick the right homes, and maybe register some folks to vote in the process.

Bushism

"It would be helpful if we opened up ANWR (Arctic National Wildlife Refuge). I think it's a mistake not to. And I would urge you all to travel up there and take a look at it, and you can make the determination as to how beautiful that country is."
—George W. Bush, Washington, D.C.,
March 29, 2001

Resources

For tips on walking door-to-door, see Chapter 22, Walking Door-to-Door.

Voter registration forms: fec.gov/votregis/vr.htm.

For bumper sticker suggestions, see Chapter 12, Your Car as a Moving Billboard.

Mail-in ballot request forms: nased.org/statelinks.htm.

Get a "Pants on Fire" car window decal and "Show George the Door, Vote 2004" or "Anybody but Bush" sticker at showgeorgethedoor.org—where you can also get a holder for voter registration and mail-in ballot request forms.

Remember, before washing dogs or cars for cash, find the applicable fundraising rules from the group or candidate you want to support.

★ MUSIC AND POETRY ★

24. *SONGS IN THE KEY OF REGIME CHANGE*

Even those of us who can't carry a tune should sing to inspire people to vote. It's fine to be out of key if it helps throw Bush out of the White House. Bush's policies have been out of key for four years.

People love live music, especially with humor. And funny songs leave a lasting impression. People can't get them out of their heads, which is exactly what we want.

Writing your own music parodies is easy and fun. We once wrote a rap song to promote trimming the Pentagon budget and investing the money in other priorities, like education and health care. We sang it at parties and meetings, and it was fun. And it's the only rap song we know that rhymes "fourteen million kids in schools that are decrepit" with "You tell me there ain't nothin we can do to he'p it."

Here are three anti-Bush parodies that we wrote with the help of Jason's wife, Anne Button. Stand up and sing them whenever you can. Or, better still, create your own. Once you get started, it's hard to stop.

Take Bush Out of the White House
(To the tune of "Take Me Out to the Ball Game")

Take Bush out of the White House,
Take him back to the ranch,
Now that it's 2004
It's time to show George Bush the door.
And it's vote, vote, vote for the Democrats;
If they don't win we're to blame.
He's too dumb to be president
And he's oh, so lame!

Liar
(To the tune of Bruce Springsteen's, and later the Pointer Sisters' "Fire")

I'm ridin' in my car, I turn on the radio;
I want to hear the truth, you just say "no."
I say I don't trust you, and your pants are on fire
The facts you twist, ooh, liar.
On Election Day, we're sendin' you home.
You say you wanna stay, we say Crawford's where you're goin'
You trumped up this war; now we're in a quagmire,
And the voters are pissed, ooh, liar.
You stole the votes right from the start
And cut Head Start with a cold, cold heart.
Your war chest's full but you're a fool
And now it's time to end your rule...
Well, home you go and don't forget, you're no unifier.
And baby, you can bet, you're gonna be fired.
It's time for you to split, and for you to retire,
You're gonna be dismissed, ooh, liar.
George Bush is a liar...
Now we're in a quagmire...
His pants are on fire...

I Bomb Iraq
(To the tune of Paul Simon's "I Am a Rock")

Election Day, in a deep and dark
November;
I am a bonehead.
Smirking from my window to the streets below
I wonder why my polls have sunk so low.
I bomb Iraq,
I am a liar.
I've built wars,
For corporations mighty
That none may investigate.

I have no need of evidence; to find it's such a pain.
I'd rather do some stretches and go train.
I bomb Iraq,
I am a liar.
I have Ashcroft
And my Cheney to protect me;
I am shielded by my daddy's friends,
I make things go boom, send soldiers to their doom,
I have a trust but no one should trust me.
I bomb Iraq,
I am a liar.
And Iraq is a shame
And this liar still denies.

You get the point. Find a song you like, or at least one that's fairly well known, and rewrite away.

If your muse can't be found, there's also a world of song parodies on the Web. One Web site has over a thousand anti-Bush parodies. Often, along with scathing lyrics that you can sing, you can click on a "MIDI-Link," which gives you an instrumental piece to sing to. The Resources section of this chapter lists some great song parody Web sites.

 for practical, concerned, and busy people.

Forward your favorite anti-Bush song parodies to your friends along with links for voter registration forms (rock-thevote.org) and mail-in ballot request forms (activoteamerica.com). Feel free to use our parodies, or use the resources cited in this chapter.

 for anti-Bush patriots with time to spare.

Sponsor or host a singing party. Print out copies of your chosen parodies beforehand, enough for all your guests. (They also make great party favors!) You can download lots of background instrumental tracks from the Internet (MIDI files), or better still, find someone who can pick out familiar tunes on the piano or guitar. Then have everyone gather round for a good old-fashioned sing-along. Have voter registration and mail-in ballot request forms on hand.

 for the anybody-but-Bush guerilla.

Call in to a local talk radio show and sing your anti-Bush song live on the radio. Do it solo, a cappella, or with back-up, vocal or instrumental or both. Or try Guerilla Karaoke, not the oxymoron it may seem: Armed with your anti-Bush song parody lyrics, go to your local karaoke bar. Request the karaoke background music, and belt your parody out. Feel free to distribute lyrics around the bar for others to join in.

You can also take your parody lyrics to a local band and ask them to perform a cover using your lyrics. Create a CD with local performers singing these songs.

Bushism

In 2004
(by Dimpled Chad & the Disenfranchised,
to the tune of the Beatles' "When I'm 64")

Do you recall all the pledges I made

Just four years ago?

A uniter, not divider, I'm no partisan clone

Please vote for me 'cause I'll change the tone.

Now that it's clear that my words were untrue,

Will you show me the door?

Do you still believe me

Or will you relieve me

In 2004?

Resources

Some of our favorite parodies come from The George Dubya Bush Songbook (bootnewt.tripod.com.bushsong.htm). The granddaddy of anti-Bush song parody Web sites, this one has more than 1,500 songs, in all different genres. For R&B, we like "Ain't No Surplus Cause It's Gone" (to Bill Withers' "Ain't No Sunshine When She's Gone"); for disco, there's "I Will Connive" (to Gloria Gaynor's "I Will Survive"). You can spend hours at this site.

Madeline Begun Kane's Web site (madkane.com/musichumor.html) includes such hits as "All I Want is a New Regime" (to "Wouldn't it be Loverly"), "Don't Cry for Dick's Halliburton" (to "Don't Cry for Me, Argentina"), and "I'm Dubya the President" (to "I'm Popeye the Sailorman").

The Georgy Bush Project (georgybush.com/lyrics.html) has some hilarious parodies like "(I Can't Get No) Enron Pension" (to the Rolling Stones' "Satisfaction"), and "Fun, Fun, Fun ('Til John Ashcroft Takes Our Freedoms Away)."

If you'd like to hear a recorded parody, try "American Way," a five song-CD by Dimpled Chad and the Disenfranchised (dimpled-chad.net), which features such classics as "The Illogical President Song," to the tune of "The Logical Song," by Supertramp: "At 9 p.m. I go to sleep, since questions run too deep, for such a simple man." You can order this CD online for $9.95, or read the entertaining lyrics and sing it yourself.

The Raging Grannies (raginggrannies.com) have been performing song parodies since well before there was a Bush presidency to end. Their Web site has instructions on how to form your own Raging Grannies parody-singing group. You don't even have to be a grand-mother.

25. DJs TO RE-DEFEAT BUSH

One evil perpetrated under Bush has been his stepped-up support for media monopolies, which squash independent and diverse music programming. Bush's backing of the continued merging of giant TV news corporations, for instance, shows where his loyalties lie.

An example of media monopolies at their worst is the current state of radio in America. News on pop stations has all but disappeared, and music is packaged and distributed according to the corporate formula du jour, leaving creative and independent voices without much of an audience.

In the aftermath of the attacks on the World Trade Center, Clear Channel Communications, the Texas-based company that owns about 1,170 radio stations nationwide, circulated to its stations a list of about 150 songs and asked its stations to voluntarily avoid playing them. The list included some clearly insensitive songs, such as the Gap Band's "You Dropped a Bomb on Me," as well as downright puzzling ones: Louis Armstrong's "What a Wonderful World," the Beatles' "Ticket to Ride," Cat Stevens' "Peace Train," the Drifters' "On Broadway," and even John Lennon's "Imagine." Given that Clear Channel reaches an astounding 54 percent of the U.S. population every week, a lot of people were "protected" from hearing a lot of songs.

The pseudo-censorship extends beyond Clear Channel. Country superstars the Dixie Chicks were dropped from many U.S. radio playlists after one of the singers criticized President Bush's stance on Iraq. Airplay for the group dropped on all U.S. radio stations by about a fifth in a seven-day period.[1] Whether the boycott was influenced by pressure from big media parent companies or not is open to debate, but, as Bruce Springsteen put it, "For them to be banished wholesale from radio stations, and even entire radio networks, for speaking out is un-American.

---

[1] Gary Younge, "Anti-Bush Remark Hits Band CD Sales," *The Guardian*, March 20, 2003.

The pressure coming from the government and big business to enforce conformity of thought concerning the war and politics goes against everything that this country is about—namely, freedom."[2]

Nonetheless, there are still some radio stations around the country that will play a song for you, if you ask.

Artist	Song	Genre	Album
Ani DiFranco	Self-Evident*	Poetry	So Much Shouting, So Much Laughter
Beastie Boys	In a World Gone Mad	Rap	Slated for release on new album in June 2004; check beastieboys.com
Billy Bragg	The Price of Oil*	Folk rock	Previously unreleased
Coldplay	Politik	Alternative	A Rush of Blood to the Head
Black-Eyed Peas	Where is the Love?	Hip-hop	Elephunk
Crass	The Unelected President*	Punk	Previously unreleased
Dixie Chicks	Any	Country	Home, Fly, Wide Open Spaces, etc.
George Michael	Shoot the Dog	Crap	Single
John Lennon	Imagine	Rock	Imagine
John McCutcheon	Hail to the Chief, The List	Folk	Hail to the Chief! (The album is available only online or at concerts, but you can download the songs for free at folkmusic.com.)
John Mellencamp	To Washington	Folk rock	Trouble No More
Lenny Kravitz	We Want Peace	Rap	Available as a free download at rockthevote.org

2 CNN, "Entertainment: Chicks Defiant With Interview, Nude Cover," November 24, 2003 (CNN.com).

Artist	*Song*	*Genre*	*Album*
Life	Bush & Blair°	Hip-hop	From 12-inch of same name
Madonna	American Life	Pop	American Life
Merle Haggard	That's the News	Country	Haggard Like Never Before
Michael Franti and Spearhead	Bomb the World	Soul, R&B	Everybody Deserves Music
Willie Nelson	What Ever Happened to Peace on Earth?	Country/ Western	Single
OutKast	B.O.B.(Bombs Over Baghdad)	Hip-hop	Stankonia
Pearl Jam	BushLeaguer	Rock	Riot Act
Pennywise	God Save the USA	Punk	From the Ashes
Public Enemy	Son of a Bush°	Rap	Revolverlution
Radiohead	Go to Sleep	Rock	Hail to the Thief
Zack de la Rocha (formerly of Rage Against the Machine)	March of Death	Rap	Download on zackdelarocha.com
REM	Bad Day, The Final Straw	Rock	In Time
Rickie Lee Jones	Ugly Man	Rock	The Evening of My Best Day
Sleater Kinney	Combat Rock, Far Away	Rock	One Beat
System of a Down	Temper, A.D.D. (American Dream Denial), Boom!	Metal	Temper is a single, ADD and Boom are on Steal This Album
Torben & Jo	Money is your Blood°	Rock	Previously unreleased

°Available on the compilation CD "Peace Not War" (peace-not-war.org).

Now is the time to ask.

Here's a list of songs promoting our campaign to take back our country.

Here's what you do:

☛ Select the song you like most.

☛ Select a radio station in your area that plays that type of song.

☛ Call the radio station (get the number from the phone book) and ask for the studio line or for the DJ.

☛ Call the DJ directly and request the song.

It's best to focus on smaller or community-based stations that don't hold their DJs in a straitjacket. A Clear Channel station probably isn't your best bet.

 for practical, concerned, and busy people.

Skip this. You can find more practical stuff to do.

 for anti-Bush patriots with time to spare.

Request one song per week.

 for the anybody-but-Bush guerilla.

Sponsor those bands or individual performers who have performed anti-Bush material to come to your town.

Bushism

Clear Channel Communications
Sent a memo to their stations
Asking DJs to take care
With songs they play upon the air
That might upset, that might divide
That just might stem the growing tide

> To send the country into war
> Guess that's what the media is for ...
> —From the John McCutcheon song "The List,"
> on the CD, "Hail to the Chief"

Resources

The Web site spacechase.net/green/rock_against_bush.htm describes bands that have spoken out, acted, or sung against Bush.

Also, there is a compilation CD called "Peace Not War," available for purchase at peace-not-war.org.

See benfrank.net/nuke/Free_Peace_mp3s.html, for additional anti-Bush songs.

A "Rock Against Bush" compilation CD is scheduled for release in April 2004 (fatwreck.com). "Rock Against Bush" will include performances from punk and alternative bands Green Day, NOFX, Good Charlotte, and others. The CD will augment the "Rock Against Bush" tour and voter registration drive, scheduled for summer 2004 and run by the Punk Voter project. The Punk Voter project (punkvoter.com), a coalition of punk bands and fans, intends to "expose the Bush Administration's incredibly bad policies" and "educate, register, and mobilize over 500,000 of today's youth as one voice."

26. POETRY FOR A BETTER AMERICA

When you're promoting something, like a new President, you need to take advantage of every opportunity to say what needs to be said.

What better opportunity than a microphone waiting for someone to say something into it?

Coffee shops across our country have "open mic" poetry readings all the time. They're looking for talented poets, like you.

"What?" you say, "I'm not a poet!" Well, we're here to help.

Poetry does sometimes make people uncomfortable. It made the White House uncomfortable in February 2003, when Laura Bush cancelled a poetry symposium over fears of anti-war protests.

The discussion was to be on the works of Emily Dickinson, Langston Hughes, and Walt Whitman. But some poets indicated they would not refrain from protest about military action against Iraq.

Former U.S. poet laureates Stanley Kunitz and Rita Dove were among those who refused to attend the event. Respected poet Sam Hamill rejected his invitation and requested that his friends send him anti-war poems. He received more than 10,000 poems in less than a month, including works by Adrienne Rich, Lawrence Ferlinghetti, Grace Paley, and Robert Bly.

Hamill established "Poets Against the War," and published an anthology by the same name (Nation Press, April 2003). On the day the White House poetry forum had been scheduled to occur, more than 160 readings were performed in countries around the world during "National Poetry Against the War Day."

Talk about taking advantage of an opportunity to say what needs to be said!

Below we provide a series of poems we wrote, with serious help from Jason's wife, Anne Button. They may not be the most lyrical, and they're certainly not immortal, as they're meant to be used right now and up until November 2 and will be irrelevant after that. We have haiku, limerick, sestet, rap, and sonnet. Please use these or, better still, write your own.

You can start with haiku. They're very easy to write; just remember the 5-7-5 syllable scheme. And no rhyming is necessary. Here are a few for starters:

Bad strategery.
Misunderestimated.
Time to go home now.

I say it's faulty
George Bush's intelligence
Double entendre

And one we found on the Web (at irregulartimes.com/haiku.html):

Shrub unites us all
Could never ever divide.
Division too hard.

Or try a limerick. Here's ours:

West Texas Limerick

There once was a boy from West Texas
Who lacked in cerebral cortexes.
He insisted on war,
Now let's show him the door
Before his position shipwrecks us.

Here's a double sestet.

Cheney's Trail

They're hurtin' for certain
At ole Halliburton
Since Cheney went to D.C.
Their investments and debt stints
Are under assessments
That everyone wants to see.

They exploded, then loaded
Those contracts with no-bid;

These are the spoils of war.
But although Dick is slick
In realpolitik,
We'll vote him out in '04.

Here's a chant, possibly a rap, depending on your delivery:

Rumination

Here's the situation:
Who will have an explanation
For the coming generation
'Bout our country's isolation
And our world domination?
Now they have an expectation
That they'll get an education
Not a Head Start termination
Or a halt to conservation
Endangered species liquidation
Or the full deregulation
Of the mighty corporation.
Got enough motivation?
Now here's an invitation
To channel your frustration:
Help us take back our nation!
Organize a demonstration,
Help with voter registration,
Make a meaningful donation,
Leaflet at the subway station.
Working in combination,
Imagine our elation
When we end the occupation
Of the Bush Administration!

And, finally, a sonnet sequence:

A Two-Stanza Anti-Bush Bonanza Sonnet

Why vote Bush out? Let us count the reasons.
War of pre-emption, Bush lands on a freighter.
Evidence? Exit? These are all treasons—
Bush says to Strike first, Ask questions later.
Tax cuts for the rich! The top one percent!
Let's go out and squander the surplus
More for the war? Consider it spent!
A growing deficit can't deter us.
Let's log in the forests, drill in the arctic,
We'll add exemptions to the Clean Air Act
Big polluters can make all the larks sick
And we'll get more money from their PACs.
> *These policies from the Bush White House team*
> *Compel good voters to end their regime.*

Let's count some more reasons, there's plenty there:
How about Cowboy Diplomacy?
Our only friends left are Sharon and Blair—
Why is this cowboy still roaming free?
He's all for Big Business, Deregulation,
He wants to promote a lunar landing
And unfunded mandates in education
Like Leaving No Child Left Standing.
As for intelligence, something seems queer,
His dearth of it, yes, but what's more
With Bush the buck stops anywhere but here—
Now voters should show him the door.
> *The reasons to vote him out seem to amount*
> *To far too many for any to count.*

for practical, concerned, and busy people.

Forward your favorite anti-Bush poems around to your friends and co-workers. Write your own, use one of ours, or go to the Poets Against the War Web site (poetsagainstthewar.org) for inspiration.

 for anti-Bush patriots with time to spare.

Make copies of your favorite anti-Bush poetry. Post the copies in the locker room, by the water cooler, on the bulletin board at the local coffee shop or bookstore, or on your Web site. Also, provide copies of voter registration (activoteamerica.org) and mail-in-ballot request forms (activoteamerica.com).

Get up on stage at open mic night with an original of your own, or use one of ours.

Compete in a poetry slam. This is a competition in which poets perform their work and are judged by members of the audience, based on the poem's content and the poet's delivery.

 for the anybody-but-Bush guerilla.

Organize a poetry reading at a local coffee shop, independent bookstore, college campus, local theater, musical venue (as a warm-up act, perhaps), art gallery, private home, or public park. Bring voter registration forms and absentee ballots so that, after you've inspired your audience, you can help them take action.

Poets Against the War has a useful document on its Web site titled "Poetry Reading How-To's" (poetsagainstthewar.org/createreading.asp) that provides step-by-step advice on finding a venue, organizing the poets, getting publicity, and what to do at the actual event.

Bushism

Call And Answer

by Robert Bly

Tell me why it is we don't lift our voices these days
And cry over what is happening. Have you noticed
The plans are made for Iraq and the ice cap is melting?...
How come we've listened to the great criers—Neruda,
Akhmatova, Thoreau, Frederick Douglass—and now
We're silent as sparrows in the little bushes?

Resources

Poets Against the War provides many anti-war poems on its Web site (poetsagainstthewar.org), from which you can also order the anthology of poems, *Poets Against the War*, Nation Press, April 2003. The site also provides a search tool to find poetry readings in your area.

You can locate poetry slams in your area at poetryslam.com/venues.htm.

One-Hundred Poets Against the War (nthposition.com) provides several different publications of poems that were designed to be printed off, copied double-sided, and distributed as chapbooks. All the contributors donated their poems, so you can download the books without copyright infringement.

There's also Poets for Peace (crixa.com/muse/unionsong/reviews/peace/poets.html).

For anti-Bush haiku, try irregulartimes.com/haiku.html.

Order a "Poets Against Bush" bumper sticker at cafeshops.com/irregulargoods.8688366 for less than $5. They offer bulk discounts; consider getting one for every poet at your reading.

★ USE YOUR WORDS ★

27. HOW TO TALK TO BUSH SUPPORTERS

There are two types of Bush supporters:

☛ The hopeless variety, whose loyalty to Bush and the Republicans never wavers, even as Bush puts the health of the republic and the planet in jeopardy.

☛ The ones who have reservations about the President's record and could possibly vote against him in November. Perhaps they agree that he turned out to be a different President than what was advertised during the last election.

It's the second category that you should spend your time talking to, leaving the first group to play with their Anne Coulter dolls in peace.

In the 2004 election, political experts say that the country is so polarized about Bush that there are fewer people than usual who are unsure about whom they will vote for. There are fewer swing voters because more voters than normal have already made up their minds.

Does this mean you should stop talking politics with Bush supporters? No. But it does mean that you probably don't want to spend too much of your limited time at it.

First, Find the Right Setting for Productive Dialog

Talk about Bush in an atmosphere where two-way communication is mostly likely to occur. Too often, political discussions happen at random and turn into cock fights when they don't need to. Be deliberate about when and where you talk about Bush.

☛ **A relaxed environment.** An informal social environment, with drinks and food, is the ideal place to start a gentle political discussion with someone who might disagree with you.

☛ **The personal touch.** Don't rush into talking about Bush. Begin your conversation by chatting about personal topics—like your families or workplace challenges—and then bring in your real agenda.

☛ **Adjust your attitude.** It's hard to look at Bush and not wonder who in their right minds could support the guy. But try to look at Bush supporters this way: They are not inclined to question authority, and when they watch Bush on TV, they believe what he says. And if you believe Bush, then much of what you hear is good stuff.

☛ **Highlight your areas of agreement.** As often as possible, tell your target Bush supporter when you agree with him or her—and when he or she makes a good point (if this is true—there's no need to be gratuitous).

☛ **Ask a lot of questions.** When you ask a question during a conversation, you not only show your open-mindedness, but you will also find out which issues you should emphasize as you make your case against Bush.

☛ **Don't try to win the argument.** As Julie Ristau, co-publisher of *Utne Reader* wrote, "conversation is not a competitive event." Don't turn your conversation into an argument with a winner and a loser. Your goal is to plant seeds of doubt, which may grow as the election approaches.

Pick Issues that Appeal to Moderate Republicans and Unaffiliated Voters

Prominent Republicans in Congress have joined Democrats in blocking some of the worst elements of the Bush agenda.

So, in trying to convince moderates to jump from the Bush ship, pick issues that have a track record of appealing to alienated Republicans. This means you should probably focus on domestic issues, rather than foreign policy.

☛ **Economy and Tax Cuts.** Many moderate Republicans are social-ly liberal but fiscally conservative. This means that they align with Democrats on stuff like Head Start, a woman's right to choose, civil rights, and other traditionally liberal social issues. But they favor smaller and leaner government, with no deficit spending. For many fiscal conservatives, Bush has been a disaster.

What You Can Say: I understand why you think cutting taxes is a good thing, but President Bush has done so *irresponsibly*. His tax cuts are heavily tilted toward lining the pockets of the richest five percent of the population and have created huge deficits that will plague future generations. Yes, the economy has been slow and we spent over $100 billion on the war, and much of the economic downturn may not be Bush's fault, but Bush has pro-duced the largest deficit in U.S. history—$500 billion or more. That looks like the work of a free-spending liberal, not a fiscally conservative Republican.

☛ **Environment.** Moderates support environmental protection. That's one reason why Bush plays lip service to it, with proposals like the "Clear Skies Initiative." But in reality Bush is vulnerable on environmental issues because he's been the most anti-envi-ronmental President since the environmental movement was born.

What You Can Say: Look, if we don't protect the environment, what kind of world are we going to pass on to future genera-tions? Bush's "reform" of the Clean Air Act, signed by flaming liberal Richard Nixon, will allow millions of tons of more pollu-tants into the air. Bush has sided with the fossil fuel industry whenever possible—on drilling for oil in our oceans and in the Arctic National Wildlife Refuge in Alaska. He wants to pollute our air, cut down our forests, and drill for oil anywhere, regard-less of its beauty or importance. A true "conservative" wants to conserve and protect the environment. Bush is not conservative at all in this sense.

☞ **Choice.** The right to choose to have an abortion is one of the issues that's tearing apart the Republican Party. The right wing is militantly anti-abortion, while moderates—even Republicans in Congress—are pro-choice.

What You Can Say: The choice to have an abortion or not should be made by women, based on their own morals. Bush will likely select two or more judges for the U.S. Supreme Court during his next term. If these judges oppose abortion, which is likely, then it's almost a certainty that Roe v. Wade will be overturned during Bush's second term. If this occurs, the states will decide whether abortion remains legal, and some states are sure to outlaw it. The poor would then be forced to seek illegal abortions, involving serious health risks—including death—and the rich would still find access to safe abortions in other countries or states. This is wrong for America.

These are the issues that we think are the most likely to appeal to moderate voters. But don't limit yourself to these issues only. Read through Part 4 of this book, Factual Ammunition: A Bite-Sized Summary of the Bush Record and see if any of the issues we've listed there are appropriate for the people you are talking to.

 for the practical, concerned, and busy person.

Buy your Republican friends a "Pack of Lies" deck of cards. Bush's record of lying sits particularly poorly with upstanding Republicans. The "pack of lies" includes fifty-two lies Bush has told with a cited "truth" that will incense honest citizens of all political stripes. Get them at showgeorgethedoor.org.

 for anti-Bush patriots with time to spare.

Think of a person, and take deliberate action. Among all the people you know and see as part of your normal life, including your family, both immediate and extended, is there one person who voted for Bush last time around who may change his or her tune in round two? If so, next time you intersect with them, at a family gathering or social event of some kind, talk to them as outlined above.

for the anybody-but-Bush guerilla.

Skip this one. Bush supporters are not likely to respond well to guerillas or a guerilla action.

Bushism

"I understand politics, and I know there's gonna be a lot of verbage."—George W. Bush, Crawford, Texas, January 2, 2003

Resources

If you have a question about the candidates' positions on any issue, call Project Vote Smart's free nonpartisan voter hotline (888-868-3762) or visit its Web site (vote-smart.org).

For talking points on a range of issues, visit the Web site of the non-partisan Center for American Progress (centerforamerican-progress.org).

For environmental and economic issues, you'll find good information from the Natural Resources Defense Council (nrdc.org), Environment 2004 (environment2004.org), which was established to draw attention to Bush's dismal environmental record, and United for a Fair Economy (ufenet.org).

28. HOW TO TALK TO YOUNG OR APATHETIC PEOPLE

A lot of apathetic people look at politics and see hopeless corruption by special interests. They say that voters are ill-informed and manipulated by advertising and the media. And what difference does an election make anyway, they ask. Look at Florida. We're living in the Dark Age, as Jason's nonvoting ex-brother-in-law puts it.

All these statements—and others like them—are true, to varying degrees, and we always acknowledge this, if we're talking to someone who thinks politics is a waste of time.

Instead of arguing about how bad the political situation is, we try to steer the conversation to 1) key issues and common values, 2) how politics is relevant to people's lives, and 3) the mechanics of how to register to vote and where to vote. For example:

☛ **The Iraq war.** You could frame a conversation about the war by expressing the value that international cooperation is our only hope for long-term international peace, global equality, and prosperity. The world might be seriously screwed up, but we'll never make progress without working with other nations. So, regardless of what you think about the war, the President's decision to abandon the United Nations in favor of waging a unilateral war with Iraq was contrary to the basic need for international cooperation.

☛ **The environment.** The need to protect the environment has wide nonpartisan support because it appeals to our core value of living with nature, not at odds with it. We will not survive if we can't figure out how to avoid destroying the world we live in. This value is put to the test when we are faced with deciding whether business interests or environmental interests should guide decisions. Bush has put business interests over environmental concerns over and over again during his presidency. Business interests claimed it would be too costly to sign the Kyoto Treaty, addressing global warming. Business interests argued that the Clean Air Act was too costly. Bush sides with business, not the environment.

☞ **Partisanship.** Apathetic people usually don't identify at all with political parties. They think both Democrats and Republicans are out to lunch. It's tempting to respond to this by saying that Bush is in outer space, but this is usually the wrong approach. Stick to values and issues, not political parties.

Talking about issues in terms of their underlying values may appeal to apathetic people and may make them dislike Bush, but it does not mean they will be inspired to vote. How to address the voting issue?

Tips for Discussing the Value of Voting

☞ Make it clear that 1) an issue or two that they care about would actually be affected by who wins the election and 2) that their vote can make a difference.

☞ To counter the common belief among apathetic people that politics is irrelevant, you need to show them how politics has a real-life impact on their lives.

☞ Offer a few facts about how important a small number of votes can be. For instance, the outcome of the 2000 Presidential election was decided by a 537 vote margin in Florida.

☞ Provide lots of information about the process of voting. Give apathetic people forms and Web sites to register to vote or to update their voter registration information. Give them forms to request a mail-in ballot. Tell them where they can go to vote in person.

☞ Don't try to guilt-trip someone into voting. While it may be a motivator for you, as an engaged voter, guilt generally doesn't do much for the apathetic voter.

☞ Offer sources of factual information about the issues. There are some great nonpartisan resources available for people who want facts about issues—both on- and off-line. (See Resources below.)

 for practical, concerned, and busy people.

Memorize one key fact about the impact of voting and one good Web site for voter registration that you could reference if you cross paths with a nonvoter. Gore lost by 537 votes in Florida, and Web sites like rockthevote.org offer easy online registration.

 for anti-Bush patriots with time to spare.

Hook up with one of the "Youth Issues" organizations listed in Chapter 6, Educate People About an Issue You Care About—and Register Them to Vote. Or bring copies of voter registration and mail-in ballot request forms to colleges, with a holder for them (from showgeorgethedoor.org).

 for the anybody-but-Bush guerilla.

By definition, the guerilla is constantly on the get-your-ass-to-the-polls warpath. Keep up the good work.

Bushism

"I'm also not very analytical. You know, I don't spend a lot of time thinking about myself, about why I do things."
—George W. Bush, aboard Air Force One, June 4, 2003

Resources

Nonpartisan voter information: In keeping with the approach of not trying to convince a young or apathetic person to vote for a specific candidate and letting them decide election questions for themselves, you might steer them to nonpartisan sources of voter information like

The League of Women Voters (dnet.org) and Project Vote Smart (vote-smart.org), which runs a free voter research hotline (888-868-3762) to answer election-related questions.

Presidentmatch.com asks site visitors questions about issues and values and matches the answers to candidates.

Youthvote.org has nonpartisan information promoting civic involvement by young people, including a "Nonpartisan Guide to Voter Mobilization."

The Campaign for Young Voters (campaignyoungvoters.org) has useful resources.

Other Web sites for youth voting issues include: rockthevote.org, declareyourself.org, votervirgin.com, and punkvoter.com.

For information on where you cast your vote on Election Day, visit declareyourself.org and type your ZIP code on the left-hand side of the home page where it says "Find Your Polling Place." Then follow the directions. Or call Project Vote Smart at 1-888-868-3762.

For information on voter registration and mail-in ballots, see Chapter 1, Register People (Including Yourself) to Vote, and Chapter 2, Vote by Mail-In Ballot.

29. THE POWER OF HUMOR

Jokes on late-night TV and comedy shows, like *The Daily Show*, are a major source of political news in America, particularly for young people. Sixty-one percent of people under thirty "regularly" or "sometimes" learn about political campaigns from comedy shows and late-night talk programs. And twenty-seven percent say they learn new information about campaigns and candidates from these shows.

That's no joke—and it's an opportunity.

We should take jokes seriously. Humor is a powerful weapon to communicate political ideas but it's under-utilized, even though, clearly, many political views are influenced by it.

Pass Bush jokes on to others as soon as you hear them (so you don't forget 'em). Send them by e-mail to friends, and forward the ones you get. Cut out political cartoons from the newspaper, and give them to your friends for posting on their barren refrigerators.

 for practical, concerned, and busy people.

Memorize a few of the most embarrassing lines Bush has said. The most practical one-liners to illustrate the ineptitude of our President are his own quotes. At appropriate moments, you could ask, how could anyone vote for a president who repeatedly says stuff like:

> "I think war is a dangerous place."
> George W. Bush, Washington, D.C., May 7, 2003

> "Rarely is the question asked: Is our children learning?"
> George W. Bush, *The New Yorker*, September 11, 2000

> "More and more of our imports come from overseas."
> George W. Bush, Beaverton, Oregon, September 25, 2000

"My opponent seems to think that Social Security
is a federal program."
George W. Bush, St. Louis, Missouri, October 17, 2000

"I know the human being and fish can coexist peacefully."
George W. Bush, Saginaw, Michigan, September 29, 2000

Many of the "Bushisms" we've included in each chapter of this book
are other examples of Bush's verbal bungling. Share them with others.

 for anti-Bush patriots with time to spare.

Learn a handful of longer jokes:

○ A man died and went to heaven. As he stood in front of St. Peter
at the Pearly Gates, he saw a huge wall of clocks behind him. He
asked, "What are all those clocks?"

St. Peter answered, "Those are Lie-Clocks. Everyone on Earth
has a Lie-Clock. Every time you lie, the hands on your clock will
move."

"Oh," said the man, "whose clock is that?"

"That's Mother Teresa's. The hands have never moved, indicat-
ing that she never told a lie." "Incredible," said the man. "And
whose clock is that one?"

St. Peter responded, "That's Abraham Lincoln's clock. The
hands have moved twice, telling us that Abe told only two lies in
his entire life."

"Where's Bush's clock?" asked the man.

"Bush's clock is in Jesus' office. He's using it as a ceiling fan."

○ George W. Bush is out jogging one morning and notices a little
boy on the corner with a box. Curious, he runs over to the child
and says, "What's in the box, kid?"

The little boy says, "Kittens, they're brand-new kittens."

Bush laughs and says, "What kind of kittens are they?"

The child responds, "Republicans."

"Oh, that's cute," W. says, and he runs off.

A couple of days later, George is running with his buddy Dick
Cheney and he spies the same boy with his box just ahead. W.

says to Dick, "You gotta check this out," and they both jog over to the boy with the box.

"Look in the box, Dick, isn't that cute? Look at those little kittens. Hey kid, tell my friend Dick what kind of kittens they are."

The boy replies, "They're Democrats."

"Whoa!" W. says, "I came by here the other day and you said they were Republicans. What's up?"

"Well," the kid says, "their eyes are open now."

 for the anybody-but-Bush guerilla.

An edgier joke for the guerilla mentality:

°   One day George W. Bush and Dick Cheney walk into a diner. A waitress walks up to them and asks if she can take their order. Bush leans close to her and says, "Honey, can I have a quickie?" The waitress is appalled and yells at the President about women's rights and storms away. Cheney then says to Bush, "George, it's pronounced 'quiche.'"

Bushism

The following poem is composed entirely of actual quotes from George W. Bush. It was compiled and arranged by *Washington Post* cartoonist Richard Thompson, and originally published as part of a January 2001 cartoon in the *Washington Post*.

Make the Pie Higher
I think we all agree, the past is over.
This is still a dangerous world.
It's a world of madmen
And uncertainty
And potential mental losses.
Rarely is the question asked
Is our children learning?

Will the highways of the Internet
Become more few?
How many hands have I shaked?
They misunderestimate me.
I am a pitbull on the pantleg of opportunity.
I know that the human being and the fish
Can coexist.
Families is where our nation finds hope
Where our wings take dream.
Put food on your family!
Knock down the tollbooth!
Vulcanize society!
Make the pie higher!
Make the pie higher!

Resources

The Internet provides a trove of Bush jokes and quotes. (Sometimes it's hard to tell the difference between a Bush quote and a joke.) A search for "Bush quotes" provides thousands of sites.

Get more embarrassing Bush quotes here: seeyageorge.com/bsh.html; lifeisajoke.com/politics22_html.htm; supak.com/bush.htm; quinnell.us/politics/2000/bushscandal2.html.

There are also calendars, daily minders, and books filled with Bushisms. Dailyhumor.net will send you a daily dose of Bush jokes. Politicalhumor.about.com has a clearinghouse of Bush jokes.

There's a nice compilation of Bush jokes on Democrats.com. Click on "COMMONS" on the left of the homepage and then on "Bush Jokes!"

★ TARGET: BUSINESSES ★

30. *RELIEVE OURSELVES OF BUSH*

To elect a President who is not a complete disaster for our nation and the world, we have to find a captive audience to hear the facts about our embarrassment in the White House. What better place than a bathroom? People have to go there, and once inside, they have to stay in one place for at least a few minutes, if not much longer, depending on their metabolism, dietary factors, and how much they like to hide in the bathroom.

 for the practical, concerned, and busy person.

Drop off voter registration forms. Leave voter registration forms and mail-in ballot request forms on toilet backs or sink counters for people to take. See Resources below.

 for anti-Bush patriots with time to spare.

Bathroom crawl. Make a night of it with your friends and take voter registration forms and mail-in ballot request forms to bathrooms all over town. While you're in bars and restaurants, drop off some "Show George the Door" coasters (showgeorgethedoor.org).

 for the anybody-but-Bush guerilla.

For guerillas, bathrooms are the perfect place to take a break from a stuffy party. And bathrooms have that anarchic reputation, so beautifully symbolized in bathroom graffiti, that guerillas love. So, it's not surprising that there are plenty of guerilla options in the rest stops:

Wipe Bush out of office with toilet paper. We all have to use it. It might as well communicate something useful. Custom toilet paper, featuring "BUSH WIPE" will get attention. It's expensive, for toilet paper, however, so you'll probably want to use it sparingly. (Find it at whatpresident.com.)

"Urinal Screens" with a message. As you know, men just stand there while they pee, usually looking at a blank wall. Talk about a captive audience! Here's how to get their attention. You can customize "urinal screens," those plastic covers on the bottom of men's urinals that hold deodorizers and stop unwanted objects from heading down the drain. Replace existing screens with "Re-Defeat Bush" ones. See Resources below.

Moving over to the sink, you can put "Wash Your Hands of Bush" stickers on paper-wrapped bars of soap, and place them by the sink. For stickers to place on the soap wrapper, use regular mailing labels you can find at any office supply store. Write "Vote Bush Out" slogans on them.

Bushism

"There's an old saying in Tennessee—I know it's in Texas, probably in Tennessee—that says fool me once, shame on— shame on you. Fool me—you can't get fooled again." —George W. Bush, Nashville, Tennessee, September 17, 2002

Resources

Voter registration forms: fec.gov/votregis/vr.htm.

Mail-in ballot request forms: nased.org/statelinks.htm. (Click on your state.)

Anti-Bush toilet paper: whatpresident.com.

Custom urinal screens: freshproducts.com makes custom urinal screens, and it even has screens where the message magically appears when used.

Hotel-sized soap: hotelsupplies-online.com.

For "Show George the Door" coasters and holders for mail-in ballot request forms and voter registration forms, visit showgeorgethedoor.org.

31. ANOTHER BUSINESS FOR VOTER REGISTRATION

Here's a way to create visible, tangible, evidential, irrefutable proof that we are not a mere campaign for a new President but a broad movement for revitalized democracy and general sanity.

Just as your body, house, car, and pet—even an apathetic one—can be put to use in the name of the movement (as described elsewhere in this book), so can your business or the business of someone you know.

Businesses often choose to stay out of politics for fear that backing one candidate would alienate some of their customers who support the other candidate. But what does a business have to lose from wearing democracy on its sleeve—or in this case, its front window?

From the standpoint of community organizing, businesses hold a place of high esteem and legitimacy. And, more importantly, they are a good way to communicate to a specific group of people. For example, record stores and coffee houses cater to a young clientele, while a shop offering second-hand baby clothes would attract the soccer-mom demographic.

But what can businesses do? How about promoting voter registration with a small sign in the windows of their establishments?

 for practical, concerned, and busy people.

Try to convince one business to put up an Another Business for Voter Registration sign in its window. Just download the Another Business for Voter Registration sign from showgeorgethedoor.org and ask a business to place it in the front window. Also ask if it will offer customers voter registration and mail-in ballot request forms. Offer them a holder for these forms as well. See Resources below.

ANOTHER BUSINESS —for— VOTER REGISTRATION

Download this sign from showgeorgethedoor.org, copy it, and ask local businesses to post it in their windows.

Credit: John Boak (boakart.com)

 for anti-Bush patriots with time to spare.

MEDIA FRIENDLY: Find three businesses to put up the sign and hold a "5 Percent Day." Find three or more businesses, preferably close to one another, to hold a "5 percent for Voter Registration" day, during which 5 percent of gross sales are donated to organizations working on voter registration. See Chapter 1, Register People (Including Yourself) to Vote. It may be up to you to spread the word about the 5 percent, so that both the businesses involved and the planet can benefit from the action.

 for the anybody-but-Bush guerilla.

Find a business to put up the sign. Guerillas may not like giant corporations, but they can relate to the people who run small businesses. Like small business owners, most guerillas are entrepreneurs and risk takers. So, download some signs and voter registration forms and take them to your favorite small business establishments.

Bushism

"I understand small business growth. I was one."
—George W. Bush, February 19, 2000

Resources

Get your free downloadable "Another Business for Voter Registration" sign at showgeorgethedoor.org. Make copies.

Get mail-in ballot request forms from fec.gov/votregis/vr.htm and absentee ballot request forms from activoteamerica.com.

Get holders for these forms from showgeorgethedoor.org.

The nonpartisan group Business Leaders for Sensible Priorities (sensiblepriorities.org) provides information about social issues from a business perspective.

The nonpartisan Social Venture Network (svn.org) is another good resource for businesses that try to do the right thing.

Businesses for Social Responsibility (bsr.org) promotes socially responsible business practices.

32. BARS FOR SOCIAL CHANGE

At the root of our democracy is the public house. Okay, there may be a few other things like freedom of speech and equality, but it is hard to deny the importance of pubs and taverns in our nation.

During the Revolutionary War, George Washington won hearts and minds while politicking over pints in pubs. A battlefield headquarters in Lexington was set up in a tavern. The Colonial Army gave away beer as a method of recruitment. Even the delegates of the new Congress in Philadelphia welcomed beer into Independence Hall.

If leaders of our own revolution weren't above hanging out in local establishments, imbibing and debating the path of our nation, we shouldn't be either.

Like coffee shops, bars can be a great place to talk politics with strangers. People are often looking for something to talk about and are loose enough to push their boundaries a bit—but hopefully not so loose that they lose their boundaries altogether and punch you.

Also, you may find allies in the owners of bars, particularly independent ones. They may join with you in doing something good for the big world beyond the barstool.

 for practical, concerned, and busy people.

Order some coasters for someone else. You're probably too busy to hang out in bars. But most of us know at least one person who goes to bars. How about buying some coasters for this person to bring to the bar? Get 'em at showgeorgethedoor.org.

 for anti-Bush patriots with time to spare.

MEDIA FRIENDLY: Happy Hour for voter registration. Find a friendly neighborhood bar owner who wants to have fun and register people to vote. Here's your proposal: You bring in your computer and printer to the bar during happy hour on an appointed day. You hook up the modem and printer, and offer people a free beer, courtesy of the democracy-supporting establishment, if they register to vote or request a mail-in absentee ballot. All they have to do is fill out the handy form on your computer (rockthevote.org), print it out, sign it, put it in the envelope that you provide, and address it. They hand the sealed envelope to the bartender for the free beer. Have mail-in ballot request forms available as well. (Advertise the event in the neighborhood with flyers and posters and, of course, in the bar with cards and whatever else is appropriate.) If you don't like booze, try this at a coffee shop, as explained in Chapter 33, Cyber Cafés for Voter Registration.

 for the anybody-but-Bush guerilla.

Pub crawl. The guerilla, ever aware, looks out across a bar and sees the following: a nervous guy talking to a cute single, a dude waiting for a slow bartender, a woman waiting for her friends to come back from the bathroom. What do they all have in common? The guerilla will observe that they all read the bar coasters. So, you guerillas, order "Show George the Door" coasters and napkins and hit the bars. (Ben suggests combining this pub crawl with a "bathroom crawl," described in Chapter 30, Relieve Ourselves of Bush, since he finds that he uses both in the same evening.)

Bushism

"It was just inebriating what Midland was all about then."
—George W. Bush, from a 1994 interview, as quoted in
First Son by Bill Minutaglio

Resources

"Show George the Door" coasters and napkins: showgeorgethedoor.org.

Custom matchbooks: absorbentprinting.com is a place we found on the net that will print one case of 2,500 matchbooks at a time.

Mail-in ballot request forms: activoteamerica.com.

Voter registration forms: fec.gov/votregis/vr.htm.

33. CYBER CAFÉS FOR VOTER REGISTRATION

Lots of coffee shops have a great tool for defeating Bush in 2004: computers with Internet access, allowing people to register to vote via Web sites like yourvotematters.org. See Chapter 1, Register People (Including Yourself) to Vote.

And even better, owners of independent coffee shops, who are often known to be liberal minded, might get involved, if we offer them reasonable ways to help—which, it turns out, they are in a good position to do. They have a regular clientele, they often hold events anyway, they have computers on their premises, and they are looking for fun ways to market their businesses.

Coffee shop owners might not go for a Bush-bashing event or a fundraiser, but they might jump at the chance to put their cyber café to work for voter registration.

 for practical, concerned, and busy people.

Drop off forms at the coffee shop. When you're picking up your morning cup of joe, leave a stack of voter registration forms and mail-in ballot request forms. (See Resources below.)

 for anti-Bush patriots with time to spare.

MEDIA FRIENDLY: Free coffee for voter registration. Try to convince the owner of a cyber café to offer a free cup of coffee to everyone who registers to vote in his or her coffee shop via yourvotematters.org or some other nonpartisan online voter registration project. To do this, the owner—or you—would provide a printer for the computer (often, computers in cyber cafés do not have printers), pens to sign the printed voter registration form, envelopes for sending the form to election officials, and stamps for postage. In exchange for handing the addressed and stamped envelope to the barista, citizens get the free java. Promoting the coffee giveaways within the coffee shop (with fliers and simple posters) might be good enough, but you could also distribute posters and fliers in strategic locations.

for the anybody-but-Bush guerilla.

Sticker the computers in cyber cafés. The guerilla ensures that his or her target gets the information they need when they need it most. Put this principle to work by pasting "Register to Vote at www.RockTheVote.org" on the computers in all the cyber cafés in your town, with the permission of the owner. Sorry, these stickers do not exist. But you're a guerilla, make your own. Any small white sticker is waiting to be put to use for the betterment of humanity.

Bushism

"See, one of the interesting things in the Oval Office—
I love to bring people into the Oval Office—right around the corner from here—and say, this is where I office."—George W. Bush, Washington, D.C., February 18, 2004

Resources

Voter registration forms: Print the form for your state from activoteamerica.com.

Mail-in ballot request forms: Print the form for your state from nased.org/statelinks.htm.

Holder for voter registration and mail-in ballot request forms: showgeorgethedoor.org.

★ GET MEDIA COVERAGE ★

34. *WRITE LETTERS TO MEDIA OUTLETS*

If you're reading this book, you are probably concerned about a lot of what you hear in the media. So are we. Here's a suggestion: Until November 2, put your anger at the news media aside and try to use media outlets in the campaign to get people to vote and elect a better president.

Respond to the day's news with a letter, e-mail, or fax. Let's send a barrage of letters to our country's media outlets, which have an enormous impact on voters. And journalists say that the letters section of the newspaper is one of the most popular in the paper.

Even the most right-wing newspapers and TV shows accept letters advocating different political positions. Your letter imploring people to vote, pointing out the latest Bush lie, or urging fellow citizens not to vote for Ralph Nader stands a decent chance of getting published or aired, especially if you submit it to a local media outlet.

The keys are to:

☛ Keep your letter short (no more than 200 words).

☛ Respond to a specific article in the newspaper or a piece on radio or TV.

☛ Make sure you send your letter to the proper location.

☛ Include your name, address, and phone number.

Also, think beyond the big daily newspapers. Send letters to the local alternative weekly, the monthly neighborhood rag. Look at what's lying on the floor of the local coffee shop and give it a try. Respond to radio programs, like National Public Radio's *All Things Considered*, TV talk shows like *The O'Reilly Factor*, and articles in magazines.

SAMPLE LETTER

Dear Editor:

I hear more and more young people saying that their votes don't matter.

I wonder if they know this: If eighteen-to-twenty-five-year-olds decide to vote, it's likely that Bush will be out of office this November. Here's why: If Al Gore had gotten the same percentage of the votes of eighteen-to-twenty-five-year-olds as Bill Clinton did, Bush would have lost, regardless of the final count in Florida.

Do young people know that the next election could be in their hands?

Sincerely,

Set yourself a goal of submitting a certain number of letters between now and Election Day.

 for practical, concerned, and busy people.

One letter between now and Election Day. Starting today, how about keeping an eye out for at least one opportunity to respond to a news story with a letter. Focus on any issue (choice, Iraq War, the economy) that you already know a bit about, so you don't have to do research. When your opportunity comes, don't pass it up.

 for anti-Bush patriots with time to spare.

One letter per month between now and election day.

 for the anybody-but-Bush guerilla.

Write a letter per week. Draft letters for yourself and for friends to edit, sign, and submit.

Bushism

"Then you wake up at the high school level and find out that the illiteracy level of our children are appalling."—George W. Bush, Washington, D.C., January 23, 2004

Resources

The Democratic National Committee (dnc.org) Web site provides you with e-mail addresses for submitting letters to the editors of major newspapers. Under the "Get Local" heading on the home page, enter your state and you will be directed to a page with a heading "Your Local Media." Click here and you will be directed to a page that lists the letter-to-the-editor contacts for the major print publications in your area.

To get information by phone on how to submit letters, click on Capital Advantage's congress.org. On the left-hand side of the home page, click on "Media Guide." Click on your state on the map, and then click on the media outlet to which you want to submit your letter. Call the main number listed and ask how to submit your letter.

35. PUBLISH A GUEST COMMENTARY (OP-ED)

There's so much to say about why we need to vote Bush out in November. Letters to the editor are one great way to express your views, but the letters are kept brief, generally fewer than 200 words. To convey all that you need to, you may want to publish a guest opinion in your local newspaper. Opinion pieces are usually about three times as long as letters. That gives you more space to articulate what a disaster Bush has been.

Opinion columns, commonly called "op-eds," appear on the "opinion" or "commentary" or "editorial" pages of the paper. The op-ed page may also contain columns by the paper's regular columnists and by nationally known writers. The latter are distributed electronically to papers across the country.

Some local radio stations also accept longer commentaries, as does National Public Radio's *All Things Considered*. If your piece is accepted by a radio station, you'll read it on the air.

For local newspapers, you've got your best shot at publishing an op-ed if it relates to local or regional issues. So, for the election, you should comment on an issue that has a direct impact on your community—perhaps by comparing how the different positions of the candidates would affect your region. The National Priorities Project (natprior.org) has excellent data on the impact of Bush policies on state and local priorities.

Tips for Writing an Op-Ed

☛ Aim for 650 words.

☛ Write in the active voice with short paragraphs.

☛ Be controversial, ironic, and funny, if you can. Don't be too serious.

☞ Op-eds respond to news that's already been reported. They do not reveal new information, nor do they announce events, products, or initiatives.

Tips for Submitting an Op-ed

☞ Submit your piece via e-mail to the op-ed editor. (Get his or her e-mail address from one of the Web sites listed below, or call your target paper and ask for the op-ed editor.)

☞ Paste your op-ed below your introductory paragraph in the body of your e-mail. *Do not send the op-ed as an attachment to your e-mail.*

☞ In the body of your e-mail, write a brief paragraph summarizing your piece (e.g., In the piece pasted below, I argue....) and the credentials of the author (e.g., title and organizational affiliation with link to a Web site).

☞ Make sure your phone number is included in your e-mail.

☞ You should give the editor a week and then call to find out the status of the piece. The best time to call is early in the week and early in the day.

☞ It's best to e-mail your op-ed to one news outlet at a time.

 for practical, concerned, and busy people.

Skip the op-ed and write a letter to the editor instead. Op-eds take many hours to write and are much more difficult to publish than a one-hundred-word letter to the editor. So, for the busy person, a letter to the editor is a much better idea. And furthermore, just as many people read the letters in the newspaper as read the guest commentaries. (For tips on writing letters and a sample, see Chapter 34 on letters to media outlets)

for anti-Bush patriots with time to spare.

Write and submit an op-ed. Follow the steps above and see if you can get an op-ed published in your local newspaper. If you do, paste it into an e-mail and send it to all your friends and relatives, and ask them to forward it to all their e-mail contacts.

 for the anybody-but-Bush guerilla.

Guerillas take newspapers in their own hands. Some guerillas have written their own op-eds and inserted them into coin-operated, street-side newspaper dispensing machines. They've also "wrapped" newspapers in fake covers. Both of these activities are illegal and we do not advocate them. But we wouldn't mind if we picked up a newspaper with a special op-ed inserted in it.

Bushism

"I think war is a dangerous place."—George W. Bush, Washington, D.C., May 7, 2003

Resources

For a list of "op-ed" editors, to whom you should submit op-eds at major newspapers, read the "Quick Tips: Op-eds and Letters to the Editor" on the Communications Consortium Web site (ccmc.org), at the left toward the bottom of the home page.

You can find a list of newspapers in your area by clicking on "Media Guide" at Congress.org, then clicking on your state.

36. LOBBY YOUR LOCAL NEWSPAPER COLUMNIST

If you read your local newspapers, you're probably familiar—maybe too familiar—with the local columnists who are paid to tell us what they think monthly, weekly, or three times a week.

At the daily papers in most large cities, there's usually at least one columnist who writes about stuff you believe in. You should try to lobby this columnist to write about something useful, like electing a new President. Columnists are always looking for material, so they want to hear from readers, particularly if you've got a good story for them.

What might a good story be? What about inviting a columnist to one of the political house parties described in this book (Chapter 8, More House Party Themes) or to the "Happy Hour for Voter Registration" (Chapter 32, Bars for Social Change)?

Whatever you do, make sure you pitch columnists a local story with community characters involved, not a recitation of the issues in the campaign. Columnists are looking for local angles on national issues, and they usually want those local angles to involve people. And it's easy to understand why: the best columns tell great stories about people in the community.

Tips for Pitching Story Ideas to Columnists

☛ E-mail a one-page pitch to a columnist and follow up with a phone call the next day. Keep calling until you reach the columnist in person. Leave a voice mail message only if you are short on time.

☛ Look for columnists' e-mail addresses at the end of their columns or on the news outlet's Web site. Or call the newspaper and ask for it.

☛ On the phone, be brief. Practice your pitch in advance. You should know within a couple of minutes whether the columnist is interested.

for practical, concerned, and busy people.

If you've got an interesting local story about the election, pick up the phone and leave a message for a columnist.

 for anti-Bush patriots with time to spare.

Host a house party and pitch it to a local columnist. See Chapters 7 and 8 on house parties.

 for the anybody-but-Bush guerilla.

Home delivery to a columnist. Guerillas like to master the art of delivering propaganda discreetly. In the case of a columnist, the guerilla might skip calling and hand deliver.

Bushism

"Actually, I ... this may sound a little West Texan to you, but I like it. When I'm talking about, when I'm talking about myself, and when he's talking about myself, all of us are talking about me."—George W. Bush, *Hardball with Chris Matthews*, May 31, 2000

Resources

To find contact information for local columnists, visit Congress.org.

Kathy Bonk, Henry Griggs, Emily Tynes, *Strategic Communications for Nonprofits*, Jossey Bass, 1999.

Lawrence Wallack, Katie Woodruff, and Lori Dorfman, *News for a Change*, Sage Publications, 1999.

37. TUNE TO TALK RADIO

Given that Rush Limbaugh and his twelve million weekly listeners have come to symbolize talk radio in America, we wouldn't blame you for thinking that talk radio is so hopelessly conservative that it deserves a chapter in 50 *Things You Can Do to ELECT Bush*, but is useless for us.

If that's what you think, here's why you're wrong. First, not all the shows are conservative. It's true that talk radio tilts way rightward politically, especially the national charades like the *Rush Limbaugh Show*, Dr. Laura, and others, but at the local level there are almost always shows that are centrist or even left-leaning.

Second, the shows with conservative hosts have big audiences, and a fraction of those audiences are independent or even liberal. For example, we know progressives who are devoted Rush Limbaugh fans because they want to get their blood going during long afternoons at the job. People who drive for a living also listen to talk radio a lot.

So, calling talk radio shows, even the conservative ones, can reach a valuable audience—not just head-buried-in-the-sand Bush lovers.

And over 70 percent of registered voters who listen to talk radio vote. Talk radio attracts folks, particularly older people, who are active in their communities and want to hear from us.

To use talk radio to help send George back to Crawford, you first have to listen to it. Take in as much as you can without going crazy. This will help you make appropriate and persuasive comments when you call in.

Once you've identified a show or two that you'd like to call, formulate comments that make sense given the tenor of the show. If it's a liberal show, talk about how important it is to register to vote and tell listeners about resources like yourvotematters.org. If it's a conservative show, focus on Bush's economic record.

Tips for Talk Radio

☛ Practice your comment on a friend, and ask him or her to play the role of talk radio host and ask you questions.

☛ Mention Web sites, events, or useful resources on the air.

☛ If the host is quarrelsome, try humor as an antidote. Try to avoid getting angry and defensive. Remain calm and clear.

☛ Ask the host questions, if he or she starts shooting hostile questions at you. This can take the momentum away from a host who's attacking you.

☛ Remember, your target is not the host, but the audience. A conservative host may disagree with you, but the audience may still be influenced by your argument.

 for practical, concerned, and busy people.

Call at least one talk radio show before the election. If you're calling a liberal show, urge listeners to tell everyone they know to register to vote. If it's a conservative show, ask listeners how they can possibly support Bush again after he's created a half-trillion-dollar deficit. Use Part 4, Factual Ammunition, for background information.

 for anti-Bush patriots with time to spare.

Don't just call into talk radio shows, try to book a guest on one. To do this, first find a notable person, such as the administrator of your city's Head Start program or a local politician, who's willing to be on a talk radio show. Then, listen to as many different shows as you can, and find one that's appropriate for your guest. Call the station's main number and ask for the producer of the show. He or she will probably not answer the phone, and his or her recording will probably ask you to send guest ideas to an e-mail address. Send your guest description (a page or so listing significant credentials) to the e-mail address, and leave a voice message for the producer briefly describing your guest. If you don't hear back after a couple days, call again and leave a second e-mail and voice message. If you still don't get a response after a couple more days, try a different talk show.

 ## for the anybody-but-Bush guerilla.

Pose as a Republican. Talk radio is a great forum for free-wheeling debate, and callers are anonymous. So it's perfectly legitimate, given the spirit of talk radio, to float arguments for their own sake. And, conveniently, guerillas are masters of disguise. We all know that the best way to convince someone of something is to claim you are one of them. Combine these truisms and you've got a great action for conservative talk radio shows. Call in and claim you are a conservative Republican. You might say something like you're so upset about Bush's fiscal irresponsibility that you've decided to vote against him next time. (See Chapter 27, How to Talk to Bush Supporters for talking points.)

Ambush a talk radio show. Packs of guerillas have more of an impact than the loner. This action will be more effective if you find at least five fellow Anybody-But-Bush guerillas: The Bush campaign is targeting conservative talk radio shows to spread their message to their faithful, and they are providing these shows with regular guests from the Bush campaign and the administration. When a talk show in your area has a Bush guest on the show, you and your fellow guerillas should all call the show and lie about what you want to ask the guest—making it much more likely that you'll get on the air. Here's how you do this. When you call a talk radio show, the producer will usually ask you for the topic of your comment. You and your fellow guerillas then tell the producer that you want to thank the official for a job well done in Iraq—or something ridiculous like that. But when you get on the air, all of you ask this question: Is President Bush going to dress up in his flight suit again and tell the American people that our mission in Iraq has been accomplished?

Bushism

"I know what I believe. I will continue to articulate what I believe and what I believe—I believe what I believe is right."
—George W. Bush, Rome, July 22, 2001

Resources

The Republican National Committee has a handy feature on its Web site allowing conservatives to easily access talk radio shows. Visit georgewbush.com/GetActive/Default.aspx, enter your ZIP code and you will get contact information for talk radio shows near you.

See Robert Bray, *Spin Works*, Spin Project (spinproject.org).

38. GET NEWS COVERAGE

Throughout this book, we've marked as "media friendly" actions that could get media attention. The news media, particularly television, rarely cover ideas (e.g., register to vote online) or isolated opinions (e.g., tax cuts for the super rich are not fair). By using the actions in this book, you can transform an idea or an opinion into an event—with a visual component—that will be covered.

Here's a quick primer on how to get media coverage of your actions to help show George the door in 2004.

Step One: Observe What's Newsworthy in Your Area

To understand what's newsworthy in the mainstream media, you have to consume as much news as possible, including local TV news, talk radio, newspapers of all types, Internet bloggers, and more. If you do this, you will quickly begin to recognize the kinds of stories that appear on, say, local TV news or a particular daytime talk radio show.

With this knowledge, it will be easier for you to determine which news outlets might be interested in covering your show-George-the-door action. For example, if you do something, anything, with costumes or animals—as suggested in this book—you've got a shot at getting on local TV. The business section of the newspaper might be interested in something you do with bars or coffee shops promoting voter registration.

Step Two: Find Names of Journalists Who Might Cover Your Action

You should "pitch" your story to a specific journalist at a news outlet. (Don't just call or e-mail whoever answers the phone at your daily newspaper.) The best way to get a media list is to find one from an ally in your community who's also working to show George the door in 2004. If this is not possible, you'll have to create your own list. But it's not too difficult.

To get a journalist's name, call the news room of the news outlet that you're targeting. Ask for the name of a reporter who might be interested in your event. Here are some tips on finding the right names at the major types of local news outlets.

☛ **Daily Newspapers:** Ask for the name of the reporter who's covering the presidential campaign or for a reporter who covers politics.

☛ **Local TV News:** Ask for the name of the "assignment" editor or possibly the "planning" editor.

☛ **News Radio or Community Radio:** Ask for the news director or a news reporter.

☛ **Alternative Weeklies:** Ask for the editor or a reporter who covers politics.

☛ **Other Local Media Outlets:** Here's a list of other local news outlets—along with (in parentheses) whom to contact at each: neighborhood weekly newspapers (the editor or reporters), magazines (the editor or freelance writers), TV public affairs programs or TV talk shows (producers), news services (news editor), and pop radio (disk jockeys).

Step Three: Learn How to "Pitch" Your Story to Journalists

Once you figure out which kind of media might be interested in your story, you need to tell journalists about it. The most common way to do this is by phone—with a follow-up e-mail. (A "press conference," where journalists gather to hear an announcement from a newsmaker, is not needed for any of the actions in this book.)

The best time to call a journalist is early in the day and early in the week. Friday is often a particularly bad time to call or to hold an event that you want covered.

Practice your pitch before picking up the phone, making sure that you've got the strongest, most concise reasons why your story merits news coverage.

If you don't reach your reporter on the phone immediately, try phoning a couple of times—or more if you have time—to get through directly without leaving a message and then leave a pitch on voice mail.

Here's a sample pitch for a local TV news assignment editor or a radio or newspaper reporter:

> *You (speaking clearly):* A group of my friends and I really want more people to vote in the next election. So we're dressing up as rabbits. Do you have a minute to hear about it?
>
> *Reporter:* Like rabbits? Sure, go ahead.
>
> *You:* We've got the bunny costumes and we've made signs that say, "We're Hopping Mad and Plan To Vote." We're going to stand on the corner of Main Street and First Avenue during the noon lunch rush on Thursday, urging people to register to vote. We've got a couple of pet rabbits that we'll have on hand in case people want to see real hoppers.
>
> *Reporter:* You're going to have live rabbits there, too?
>
> *You:* Yup. We're going to try to make them hop with us. We think a lot of people are hopping mad at Bush like we are, and we want them to vote.
>
> *Reporter:* So when will this happen? How many of you are there?
>
> *You (speaking slowly):* Noon on Thursday at the corner of Main Street and First Avenue. Three of us will be hopping rabbits, but we expect a crowd of fifteen or more to cheer us on with chants like, "Hop, hop, Bush we must stop," and, "We're hopping mad, but not too sad to vote!"
>
> *Reporter:* We'll try to get someone there. Do you have any of this written down?

You: If you want, I'll send an e-mail with all the information.

Reporter: Yes, thank you. I'm jreporter@cbs.com.

You: Thanks. I'll shoot it over now.

You don't have to have a flashy event to get coverage, but if your action has less visual appeal, you'll have better luck with a newspaper reporter than with a TV one.

Step Four: Send a News Release, if Appropriate

If you think your story could be of interest to a couple of different reporters (e.g., the daily newspaper and local TV news), you should prepare a "news release," which is a one-page explanation of your "news," prepared specifically for journalists. News releases are written like news in the newspaper or on TV, with short paragraphs and quotations.

Most of the time that you dedicate to writing a news release should be spent on the headline and first paragraph. The heart of your story—as well as any visual imagery for television—should be described in the headline. If appropriate, be creative and try to grab your readers.

You can check out sample news releases on causecommunications.com.

Step Five: Make a Follow-up Call

After you send a personal e-mail or a news release to a reporter, whether you've actually spoken to him or her or simply left a voice mail message, you should call again within twenty-four hours to make sure that your e-mail or news release was received.

Step Six: Become a Master Interviewee

You should prepare to be interviewed at your action. The key to successful interviews with journalists is to keep it simple and interesting. Your goal is to stay "on message." This means that no matter what a reporter asks, you should answer with one or two central reasons why you are taking action, such as you want people to vote.

You should also develop a soundbite or two to communicate your simple messages. Soundbites are a type of speech commonly found in the news, especially TV news. They are defined by how long they take to deliver (five to twelve seconds) and the style of language they contain (action verbs). An effective way to write a soundbite is to begin with the phrase, "I'm here today...." (E.g., "We're here today in the skunk costumes because President Bush's environmental policies stink, and we want people to vote in November.") As in this example, the most quotable soundbites are linked to imagery of your event. (Another example: "The truth about the governor's position is as plain as the nose on Bushocchio.")

Tips to Be a Master Interviewee

☞ Practice answering questions in advance. Have your friend play the role of reporter. (Why are you upset with Bush? Why do you want people to vote?)

☞ Speak slowly and give brief answers to questions, without acronyms and insider jargon.

☞ Realize that it's okay to be nervous; anxiety can actually add vigor and clarity to your thoughts.

☞ Everything you say to reporters, even after the official "interview," could be used in their stories. Never assume journalists agree with you, though they will often act as if they do.

☞ If you don't have an answer to a question, say so and try to track down an answer later.

☞ Don't worry about being a "media personality." Be yourself.

Step Seven: Keep Trying

Don't be afraid. Although busy, most journalists are friendly people who want to hear from you. Be aggressive, persistent, and polite.

Just because you didn't get covered one day doesn't mean you won't make the news the next. On a slow news day, anything can be news.

Bushism

"If you want to build a big project and you can't get insurance because of what the terrorists have done for America, you can put the project aside."—George W. Bush, Oakland, California, October 14, 2002

Resources

Check out Jason's book, *Making the News: A Guide for Activists and Nonprofits*, Westview Press, 2003, for everything you need to know to get media attention.

The Spin Project (spinproject.org) has detailed information in the "Resources" section of its Web site on how to stage events and contact the news media.

★ REACH OUT ONLINE ★

39. SNEEZE BUSH BACK TO CRAWFORD

To become a Sneezer Against Bush, all you need is an e-mail address.

Sneezers are those people who pass e-mails to all their friends. We all know these types, and certainly get aggravated with them if they overdo it. But if you forward e-mails with sensitivity, maybe two to four times a month, and you forward good stuff about how to defeat Bush, your friends will love you for it—or at least tolerate you, especially if you add a good joke or, say, a link to the Bushocchio game (showgeorgethedoor.org).

After receiving your e-mail message, your e-mail contacts might forward it to their friends, and so on, spreading the e-mail from one computer to another.

This is effective because each e-mail that's passed on carries the personal endorsement of whoever forwarded it. Because the e-mail comes from a person known to the recipient, he or she will most likely pay attention to it—unlike typical unwanted and anonymous e-mail, called spam, which lands in your e-mail box. In short, an e-mail forwarded from a friend has legitimacy.

Here's what you should consider doing.

From now through November 2, forward e-mails that you receive that offer a reasonable way to help elect a new president.

For example, if you get an e-mail for a rally welcoming the Democratic candidate to your town—or protesting a visit by Bush—forward it to anyone who might be even remotely interested.

By doing this, you will be using one of the greatest attributes of the Internet. It gives you the ability, via e-mail, to disseminate essential information without relying on the media conglomerates to put it in the newspaper or on TV.

for practical, concerned, and busy people.

Send e-mails; sneeze as often as you can.

 for anti-Bush patriots with time to spare.

Build a better e-mail list and start sneezing. Set a goal of expanding your e-mail address book by fifty contacts within the next month, focusing especially on the type of person who will take action to stop Bush. Look at this as your opportunity to obtain the e-mail addresses of family, friends, co-workers, or anyone with whom you've been wanting to be in better touch.

 for the anybody-but-Bush guerilla.

Find the best things to do to defeat Bush and sneeze them. Stand back when a guerilla sneezes, because who knows what you'll catch. In this case, anybody-but-Bush guerillas should comb the Web for the best guerilla tactics to send Bush back to Crawford. (Feel free to lift a few from this book.) Write 'em up and sneeze 'em to fellow laptop warriors, wherever they may be.

Bushism

"Will the highways on the Internet become more few?"
—George W. Bush, Concord, New Hampshire,
January 29, 2000

Resources

See Chapter 49, Stay Informed About Late-Breaking Actions and Issues, for a list of organizations that will send you e-mails—which you can sneeze on to your contacts—about actions you and other sneezers can take.

40. *ADOPT A BLOGGER*

We can't ignore the mainstream media—like TV, radio, and newspapers—in our grassroots campaign to send Bush back to the private sector where he can squander his family money, instead of our tax dollars.

But, when the opportunity presents itself, we have to take advantage of nontraditional sources of information as well—like "blogs" (a contraction of the words "web" and "log").

Blogs are Web sites—or pages on Web sites—that contain a stream of information or opinion posted daily (or at least periodically) by a "blogger," who is essentially an Internet diarist.

Blogs are chatty, confrontational, gossipy, snide, irreverent, and fun, with a generous offering of links to everything—allowing you to "see the proof" when a blogger trashes another writer or a public official.

Hundreds of thousands of blogs grace the Web's blogosphere. You can find them on any topic. Some have weird themes like popculturejunkmail.com, which covers "trashy TV, British Royalty, the 1980s, toys, movies, cats, weird makeup, and more." Some have no definition at all. Others focus on politics. The Web sites of official news outlets even have bloggers.

We can disseminate our Show-George-the-Door message via the blogosphere.

To do this, we need to feed information to targeted bloggers, who are hungry for information they can post on their blogs. But it can't be just anything, because sending bloggers information that's irrelevant to their blog will just irritate them and cause them to ignore you.

Tips for Using Blogs to Spread the Word

☛ Talk back to bloggers—and do it quickly, in response to issues addressed in the blog that you are targeting. Use the e-mail address that's posted on the blog. Many bloggers liberally share comments—but they don't post everything.

☛ Be selective in choosing your target blog. Many are read by no one except the blogger and his mom. Find blogs that are well-known. (See Resources below.)

☛ First, pick your target message (like you want to increase voter turnout) and audience (like eighteen-to-twenty-five-year-olds) and action (Get voter registration and mail-in ballot request forms on the Web). Then find an appropriate blog. For a list, see Resources below.

☛ Monitor targeted blogs or use blog search engines that search blog content. (See blogcritics.org.) A search on Google.com will yield a breakdown of blogs in numerous categories.

 for practical, concerned, and busy people.

Adopt a blogger. Read a bunch of blogs and select one that appeals to a swing demographic group, like young people or seniors, or addresses a swing issue (like the environment) that resonates with you. Send relevant information to your target blogger at least a few times a month, keeping in mind the appropriate message for the audience of the blog. Subscribe to one or more of the online organizations described in Chapter 5, Help Defeat Bush in Swing States (Even if You Don't Live in One) for ideas on what to send the blogger, but you can literally send anything from suggested actions, like how to register to vote via the Internet, to where to get mail-in ballot request forms and anti-Bush gifts.

 for anti-Bush patriots with time to spare.

Adopt a dozen bloggers. You do exactly the same thing as the "Practical, Concerned, and Busy People" do above, but pick twelve bloggers instead of just one.

 for the anybody-but-Bush guerilla.

Adopt conservative bloggers: Guerillas go incognito every time they get a chance. Like talk radio, blogs are a forum for discussion, where anonymity is accepted for the sake of freewheeling democratic debate. So, find a few conservative bloggers from the lists below, pretend you are a conservative, and start sending the blogger relevant stuff, like information on the growth of the deficit, Bush's irresponsible management of tax policy and the economy, and other information that's upsetting—and convincing—to conservatives. (See Part 4, Factual Ammunition: A Bite-Sized Summary of the Bush Record.)

Bushism

"Anyway, I'm so thankful, and so gracious—I'm gracious that my brother Jeb is concerned about the hemisphere as well."
—George W. Bush, Miami, Florida, June 4, 2001

Resources

There's an entire nation of bloggers, but you can find the most widely read ones at Dailykos.com and Instapundit.com.

For a list of journalists who write blogs on the Web sites of mainstream media outlets, visit CyberJournalist.net, maintained by Jonathan Dube of the American Press Institute.

Find links to progressive bloggers at the *Mother Jones* Web site, motherjones.com/news/dailymojo.

41. FEED WEB SITES

Do you have a favorite political Web site, where you go for a jolt during the workday when the coffee is wearing off? You might be able to include it—and other Web sites—in the cause of defeating Bush.

Web sites, of course, cover the universe of issues and beyond. Most Internet news consumers visit the biggest Web sites for news and information. These include: MSNBC.com, CNN.com, NYTimes.com, ABCnews.com, USAToday.com, WashingtonPost.com, Time.com, LATimes.com, FoxNews.com, and WSJ.com. This type of Web site, from a mainstream media outlet, is a tough nut to crack in terms of pitching ideas or stories.

But there's a broad, second-tier group of sites that have a core following and are open to suggestions from surfers like you.

The owners of these sites, which are often associated with an activist group or grassroots activity, often struggle to stay current and want to receive information about stuff they *can use on their sites*. This could mean:

☛ A link to an action to help defeat Bush, like yourvotematters.org, which promotes online voter registration.

☛ A link to a Web site with relevant campaign information, like showgeorgethedoor.org.

☛ A Web-based game, like spankbush.com.

☛ A notice of an event.

☛ A link to a relevant news article.

☛ Something they could sell in their online store. (See Chapter 4, Gifts for the Election Season.)

Here's how you promote this type of stuff to a Web site:

☛ Match your suggestion to the politics of the target Web site. For example, a nonpolitical site might post a link to a site where you can register to vote online. Or a lefty site might like to hear about a link to spankbush.com.

☛ Browse your target site carefully and figure out where your ideas could be posted on the site.

☛ Scrutinize the site and find a name of someone who is either in charge of content for the site or may lead you to the person who does make decisions. This might take some fishing.

☛ Write him or her a personal e-mail note, with a link to the information that you want posted. Specify where on his or her site you think your tidbit would fit. Only suggest information that can be accessed online.

☛ Do not attach files to your notes. Attachments are seldom opened by anyone who receives unsolicited e-mail, for fear of viral attack.

☛ Follow up with a second note in a week, asking if the material was received.

☛ If you still get no response and you're feeling bold, try a phone call after your second e-mail.

 for practical, concerned, and busy people.

Join a discussion thread or message board and promote voter registration and voting by mail. Respond to Web sites that invite readers' comments, being sure to provide links to voter registration sites.

 for anti-Bush patriots with time to spare.

Nurture six Web sites. Find half a dozen Web sites and make contact with the person who's in charge of decisions about their content, as described above. Promote voter registration (your-votematters.org or another link as described in Chapter 1, Register People (Including Yourself) to Vote to them.

 for the anybody-but-Bush guerilla.

Pose as a conservative. In the interest of sparking debate where anonymity is acceptable, pretend to be a conservative who is irked at Bush's irresponsible fiscal record and deficit spending.

Bushism

"In my judgment, when the United States says there will be serious consequences, and if there isn't serious consequences, it creates adverse consequences."—George W. Bush, *Meet the Press*, February 8, 2004

Resources

Live online chats: georgewbush.com, rnc.org (check for schedules) and ask Republicans tough questions.

Message boards: There are tens of thousands, but start with the Web sites for your local newspaper. Often there is a discussion thread after an article.

42. *HOMING IN ON THE PRESIDENCY*

For you low-level techies, your "home page" is the Web site that appears after you click on the button that takes you to the Web. Your home page is what you see every time you start surfing the Web.

It takes about one minute to turn an irrelevant home page into a tool in the campaign to re-defeat George Bush.

With a few clicks of a mouse you can replace any home page (many people have msn.com or google.com as home pages) with one that provides late-breaking stuff you can use to help defeat Bush. Or you can get the latest fodder you need to win arguments about Bush.

First, select your favorite political Web site or choose one listed in Chapter 49, Stay Informed About Late-Breaking Actions and Issues.

Here's how you change the home page. This will differ depending on the type of computer and software you use. On many personal computers running Microsoft's Internet Explorer, go to the Web site that you want to be your new home page, click on "Tools," then "Internet Options." Click on "General," and then below "Home Page," click on "Current." That's it. For Macintosh, you will need use some combination of "Tools," "Preferences," and "Set-up Options," to change your home page settings.

If these instructions don't work for you, access the Web and click on "Help." Type "Home Page" in the index, and you should find instructions for changing your home page.

 for practical, concerned, and busy people.

Change the home page on your own computer, as explained above, to keep up on campaign events.

for anti-Bush patriots with time to spare.

At work, or whenever you get the chance, ask your fellow workers or others if they'd like to change their home page to keep better track of election issues. Suggest a Web site that's appropriate. Offer to change it for them.

 for the anybody-but-Bush guerilla.

Target the computers of skeptical family and friends who might consider voting against Bush. Here's how you might do this: You stay late at a party or wander into your uncle's office when you're over at his house. Slide over to the computer and make the switcheroo.

Bushism

"Sometimes it's not easy to be the friend of George W. Bush—I know that. If you know what I mean."—George W. Bush, Houston, Texas, September 12, 2003

Resources

Turn to Chapter 49, Stay Informed about Late-Breaking Actions and Issues. You'll find a good list of Web sites listed there.

★ MORE THINGS YOU CAN DO ★

43. *DON'T VOTE FOR RALPH NADER OR ANY THIRD-PARTY CANDIDATE*

Some of us love Ralph Nader. Some of us don't. Some voted for him in the last election. Some didn't. But for the 2004 elections, one thing is clear. It's time for all of us to join together to elect the Democrat so that George Bush is defeated.

Both major parties clearly have their problems. But this is the year to dump Bush, and to do that we need to vote Democratic. As we mentioned earlier, for many Republicans, Independents, and Greens, voting for the Democrat might require a powerful set of noseclips, allowing these people to have their nose plugged and hands free when they vote. If that's what you need, get them at holdyournoseandvote.com.

In the 2000 election, the number of votes for Nader exceeded the number of votes Bush beat Gore by in two states: New Hampshire and Florida. Winning either one of those states would have given Gore enough electoral votes to win the election. For an explanation of the Electoral College system, see Part 3: Voter Registration (and Mail-in Ballot) Resources and Deadlines. If fewer than 600 Nader voters in Florida had voted for Gore instead, there would be no need to show George the door today. And Nader got over 97,000 votes in Florida.

Many people don't realize that, even without winning Florida, Gore would have won the presidency if he had carried New Hampshire, where Bush won by a margin of 7,211 votes. Exactly 22,188 people voted for Nader in New Hampshire.

Given the imperative of beating Bush, it's not worth the risk to vote for a third-party candidate of any kind, Green, Libertarian, or otherwise, even if you live in a "safe" state. Every single supporter of the

Democrat will add momentum to the campaign, especially if all of us take action in addition to voting.

Also, if you support a third-party candidate in a "safe" state, the candidate's national poll numbers will rise, giving him or her national credibility and appeal that could detract from the Democrats' campaign.

It's up to all of us to convince everyone to vote Democrat this time.

 for the practical, concerned, and busy person.

If you're hyper-practical, you probably did not vote for Nader, and you should pick something else to do. Nader voters tend to hang around each other. If you didn't vote for him, you probably don't know Nader voters, and trying to find some to convince to vote Democrat would be too time consuming for you.

 for anti-Bush patriots with time to spare.

Locate at least three people who voted for Ralph Nader in 2000. Find out if these people are voting for the Democrat this time. Using the arguments above and at repentantnadervoter.com, convince them to vote for the Democrat. If they still refuse and they live in a swing state, then try to convince them to trade their vote with a Democratic voter who lives in a state that will almost certainly go to Bush or the Democrat. To do this, they have two options:

° Find someone, like a friend or relative, who lives in a "safe" state and will promise to vote for the third party candidate if the person in the swing state votes for the Democrat.

° Visit a Web site that helps facilitate vote trading as described above. One such site is votexchange2000.com.

 for the anybody-but-Bush guerilla.

Protest when Nader comes to your town. But consider orienting your protest toward Bush, not Nader, using signs like "I Love Ralph, But I Will Vote Democrat." This would send the message to Nader supporters that even people like them are voting against Ralph this time. Or you might go with a "Vote Out Bush" sign. If you want to organize such a protest, contact repentant-nadervoter.com for help.

Bushism

"My mom often used to say, 'The trouble with W'—although she didn't put that to words."—George W. Bush, Washington, D.C., April 3, 2002

Resources

See Part 2, An Election Primer: Swing States, The Electoral College, and More.

Check out repentantnadervoter.com, dontrunralph.net, or nonader.org for some good arguments against supporting Nader or any third party this time around.

In 2000, votexchange2000.com helped Nader voters "trade" their votes with Democrats in "safe" states. A similar campaign will probably take place this year.

44. TURN YOUR HOBBY (BOOK CLUB, OR TEAM) INTO A POLITICAL FORCE

We all have a passion in our lives. Some of us even find time to pursue it with others who share our interests. Although it may be difficult to tear yourself away from discussing model trains, shin splints, dropped stitches, or whatever your group usually talks about, your hobby groups can be a vehicle for a political statement.

Maybe you are in a softball, soccer, or bowling league. If you are not insulted to find your sport relegated to the hobby chapter, your team probably doesn't take itself too seriously. So why not name your team *Anybody But Bush* or the *Bushocchios* (like Pinocchio)? Your message will be printed on the league schedules and on your jerseys.

If you make beer at home, enter your libations in a homebrew contest under the name "Bitter Bush," or "Thick-Headed Bush Stout."

The same applies to county or state fairs. Why not enter a lamb in the 4-H contest that has the name, "Bush is Baaaaaddddd"?

Urge your book club to read one of the many best-selling Bush exposés—or a book on what they can do to unseat Bush, like this one.

Play poker or other card games with the "Pack of Lies" deck of cards featuring fifty-two Bush lies, the truth, and the rules for Bushingo, the new card came. (Get them at truemajorityaction.org.)

 for practical, concerned, and busy people.

Make one political statement, as explained above, with one of your hobbies or pastimes.

 for anti-Bush patriots with time to spare.

Organize your fellow hobbyists to take action. Go a step further and organize political volunteers from your hobby group. You could choose an action from this book and do it together. For example, say your book group usually gets together monthly to discuss a book. These meetings usually degenerate into gossip sessions anyway. So, suggest to the group that you dedicate the next month's meeting to an activity that will help elect a President who's literate. The members of a typical book group are probably politically aligned, but this is not the case for all hobby organizations. Your Tuesday evening jogging group may represent all political stripes. Don't let this deter you. Just ask who wants to join you, and work with whomever you get. As with a religious group, you may find that people want to be politically active, but they've never been given a comfortable way to get involved. The invitation from you, as someone they know as a fellow hobbyist, could be the perfect ticket to activate them, especially if Bush is driving them crazy.

 for the anybody-but-Bush guerilla.

Choose another action. The typical guerilla spends most of his or her time on hobbies, and as little time as possible on real life. And the guerilla's major hobby is battling for regime change. You guerillas out there live this chapter—go for it!

> ## Bushism
>
> "Sometimes when I sleep at night
> I think of (Dr. Seuss's) 'Hop on Pop.'"
> —George W. Bush, Washington, D.C., April 2, 2003

Resources

See Chapter 4, Gifts for the Election Season, Chapter 1, Register People (Including Yourself) to Vote.

Runners, visit runagainstbush.org.

45. FUN FUNDRAISING

It's going to take all kinds of fundraisers to get enough money to elect a new president—and all kinds of actions to convince people to vote. This chapter outlines ways to do both at the same time.

Remember that fundraising regulations can be complex. The easiest way to avoid breaking any rules is to decide before your fundraising event which organization or political campaign you want to raise money for. Then contact the future recipient of your donations and find out what the rules are for contributions.

The trick is to conceive of a fundraiser that's fun. Holding a "house party" with your friends is one of the best ideas (See Chapter 27, Host a House Party), but house parities are not the only option.

"Stop the Special Interest Feeding Frenzy" feast and cooking demonstration. Do you know a good cook with even better politics? If so, ask him or her to cook a meal for you and others who are willing to make a donation to attend. The money would be used to serve Bush a defeat in November.

"Not $1,000-per-Plate" dinner. We can't rely, like Bush does, on $1,000-per-plate dinners to finance the Democrat's campaign. But how about a regular price meal? You might be able to find a restaurant that will serve a dinner at cost, while your group pays full price or more. This might occur on a day the restaurant is normally closed.

"Junk Bush" yard sale. Speaking of yard sales, how about having one for regime change? What better way to utilize useless junk than for the most useful cause on the planet? And it's a nice metaphor for the task before us this election year: throwing out old junk. You could even get your friends together and have a joint sale, which is usually more fun anyway, not to mention more lucrative.

"A New Prez Would Be So Sweet" bake sale. Veterans of peace movements past probably know the beautiful poster with the kids climbing up a jungle gym and the phrase, "It will be a great day when our schools have all the money they need and the Air Force has to hold a bake sale to buy a bomber." Now, if that old poster isn't perfect for our times, what is? So, use it as a theme for a neighborhood bake sale. Sell the goodies and the poster. To order the poster, visit wilpf.org/forsale/catalog.html.

"Chase Bush Out of Office" run. You're probably thinking, no way am I organizing one of those big 5k races, like the Furry Scurry. You don't have to. Just get the word out among a small group of your friends who jog, designate a day, time, and place, suggest a donation, and you're off. Hint: If you are slow, collect the donations at the starting line. (Serious participants could collect pledges for each mile or yard that they run or walk, depending on their athletic abilities.) For ideas, visit runagainstbush.org.

Bushes *can* be beautiful. Find a group of four or so people who have nice gardens and ask them if they want to offer a tour of their gardens to help defeat Bush. Write up an invitation and ask for donations. Come and enjoy an afternoon touring the gardens. Commune with nature, enjoy some shade, smell the roses, and do your part to eliminate noxious bushes from the White House. With your donation, we can stop the pernicious Dubya weed from spreading this November.

Other ideas: **Talent Show, Fashion Show, Auction, Dance Lessons,** and **Art Show.**

At any of these events, you should have plenty of voter registration forms and candidate information. Make a big banner (use a white cotton sheet and black latex paint) or simply use cardboard signs to make sure people understand what's going on.

 for practical, concerned, and busy people.

Patronize any house party or other fundraising event, like these, that you hear about.

for anti-Bush patriots with time to spare.

Pick one of the above and do it.

 for the anybody-but-Bush guerilla.

Try satire. Guerillas have a nose for the absurd, because, as Saul Alinsky noted, "It is almost impossible to counter-attack ridicule." So try having a "Billionaires for Bush" party. See billionairesfor-bush.com for inspiration and laughs.

Bushism

"It's very important for folks to understand that when there's more trade, there's more commerce."—George W. Bush, Quebec City, April 21, 2001

Resources

For the poster with the line, "It will be a great day when the schools have all the money they need and the air force has to hold a bake sale to buy a bomber," visit wilpf.org/forsale/ catalog.html.

Also see Chapter 23, A Dog or Car Wash for a Cleaner White House, Chapter 7, Host A House Party, and Chapter 8, More House Party Themes.

46. *VOLUNTEER AT THE CAMPAIGN OFFICE*

If you're politically active, you've probably had politically apathetic people act like they're your psychologists when it comes to explaining *your* political behavior. They've probably informed you that you go to rallies and political meetings more for therapy than to really make a difference—in other words, so you can complain with other delusional people.

Okay, yes, we agree that huddling together and trying to make the world a better place with like-minded people *does feel good*. It is therapeutic to register people to vote at a street fair or to carry a "NO WAR IN IRAQ" sign at a rally.

But—and if only the apathetic could be convinced of this—political activism can also make a difference.

Take volunteering in a campaign office. We all know that elections can be won or lost by a few hundred votes. And campaigns rely on volunteers to get out the vote. Do you need any more proof that trying to convince people to vote is important?

And it's fun. Campaign offices are informal, friendly places that attract an odd mix of good-hearted folks—some of whom invariably turn out to be amazing characters—who want to have a good time and win. You don't have to be any particular type of person—like a frenetic type A personality—to fit in. There are jobs for everyone (including type A's).

And if you don't want to work at the campaign office, you can get things to do at home.

Volunteers support the basic goals of the political campaign, which, in a nutshell, are: convincing people to vote for your candidate, identifying voters who support you, and making sure your supporters actually vote.

Much of this is done by phone, using highly targeted phone lists. Volunteers—who are given phone scripts and plenty of coaching—call people on the lists. This is often called phone banking.

Probably the next most common volunteer task in a campaign is walking door-to-door, dropping off campaign materials, and talking to people. There's no better way to convince people to vote and support your candidate. That's why campaigns assign so many volunteers to doing this. (See Chapter 22, Walking Door-to-Door.)

In addition to the biggest tasks of phone banking and walking door-to-door, campaign volunteers might do any of the following tasks:

☛ Tabling at events (fairs, races, games). Campaigns aim to have tables wherever there's a crowd.

☛ Answering the phone.

☛ Delivering lawn signs to people who request them.

☛ Helping with mailings.

☛ Organizing leaflets for canvassers.

☛ Running errands, buying food, or making coffee.

☛ Recruiting or picking up volunteers.

 for practical, concerned, and busy people.

Volunteer three hours for the campaign. Though it's extremely practical, volunteering for a campaign is not for the busy person. But, precisely because it is so practical, busy people should squeeze in some time to do it anyway. Find a friend or two, and call a voter registration group or the Democratic Party office in your area and say that you've got three hours to contribute between now and Election Day. Ask when they could most effectively use your help. See Resources below for whom to call.

for anti-Bush patriots with time to spare.

Dedicate one evening a week to the campaign office. It's best, if you can, to set aside a regular time for volunteering at the campaign office. You'll get to know the staff and other volunteers better, so it will more fun. And you'll be more effective because you'll stay on top of the issues and campaign developments.

 for the anybody-but-Bush guerilla.

Guerillas form their own campaigns and should skip volunteering at the campaign office.

Bushism

"And so, in my State of the—my State of the Union—or State—my speech to the nation, whatever you want to call it, speech to the nation—I asked Americans to give 4,000 years—4,000 hours—over the next—the rest of your life—of service to America. That's what I asked—4,000 hours."—George W. Bush, Bridgeport, Connecticut, April 9, 2002

Resources

For a list of organizations to contact, see Chapter 6, Educate People About an Issue You Care About—and Register them to Vote and Chapter 5, Help Defeat Bush in Swing States (Even if You Don't Live in One).

For a list of local Democratic Party chapters, see democrats.org or call 202-863-8000.

47. YOUR PLACE OF WORSHIP

Faith gives many, many people the inspiration to work for political change. Some of America's greatest social justice movements have their roots in faith-based communities.

If you are a person of faith and attend a church, synagogue, or other place of worship, you're tapped into a powerful community that can make a difference in this election.

But when it comes to elections, most churches, synagogues, mosques, or other official places of worship cannot endorse political candidates—or oppose them—because their nonprofit tax status prohibits it. This book is clearly partisan, but there's a lot you can do that's nonpartisan that would be acceptable to your place of worship.

Even if a religious organization could get away with it legally, there are often divisions about whether engaging in partisan politics is consistent with religious principles. Some people of faith are totally committed to ousting Bush and argue that the scriptures demand it. Others are equally committed to regime change, but do not believe that their place of worship should be involved in partisan politics.

So, you may find it a bit tricky to engage your place of worship in political activities.

Here's a sample of what you can do:

Join a justice committee. If there's already a social justice committee at your place of worship, join it. Find out if there are any plans to hold events related to the November election. If the committee has no plans, suggest one from the list below or, if appropriate, from elsewhere in this book.

If there's no committee, start one. Your congregational directory is your best tool for doing this. Begin by calling people listed in it. You may find more support than you think. Getting involved in politics is scary for many people, and if you—as a member of a congregation—

call other members, you may be giving them a comfortable way to get involved, even if they have never been politically active before.

If the committee does not have power players in it—board members, donors, past leadership—try to get them involved. Activists within many congregations often do not work regularly with people who can have the most impact.

Register the congregation and others to vote. One of the most common election-related activities in the faith community is voter registration, not just focusing on the congregation. You often see faith-based voter registration tables at community events, as well.

Influence the service. Depending on the politics of your congregation leader and your denomination, you can provide him and her with information that connects issues in a campaign—including the need to vote—to religious themes. Sojourners offers a monthly online nonpartisan newsletter called "Preaching the Word," which costs $45 per year. It has biblical commentary, "organized according to the Revised Common Lectionary for Sundays, so preachers, worship leaders, pastors, and Bible study groups can easily get to the challenging heart of the scriptures."

Organize a lecture or have a guest deliver the service. The closest thing you may get to a political event in your place of worship could be a lecture. Sometimes an outside lecturer will be allowed to deliver the service. Such a lecture, even if it's less like a Michael Moore–style call to arms and more of a discussion of spirit and justice, can have a real impact on a congregation, as members—often with different political views—talk about the issues informally.

Distribute nonpartisan voter guides. Nonpartisan voter guides, listing all candidates, can be distributed in your place of worship or sent to your congregation. These guides, which compare the candidates' positions on various issues, are an excellent way to offer information about the election, without taking a partisan position. Bread for the World (breadfortheworld.org) produces a voter guide.

for practical, concerned, and busy people.

Find out if there's a social justice committee at your place of worship. If it's got something planned around the election, consider lending a hand.

 for anti-Bush patriots with time to spare.

Pick one of the options listed above and organize it. If a social justice committee already exists, join it and get active. If not, start one or get an unofficial group of your congregation together.

 for the anybody-but-Bush guerilla.

Place flyers on the cars in the parking lots of liberal churches. The church of the guerilla is often the old growth forest, though guerillas have been known to be priests, rabbis, reverends, and Imams or just about any other religious person. In any case, get mail-in ballot request forms for your state, and make a few hundred copies. (Get the form from activoteamerica.com.) Find out which large churches in your area are liberal and, on a Sunday morning this summer, place fliers on the windshields of the cars in the parking lot.

Bushism

"I couldn't imagine somebody like Osama bin Laden understanding the joy of Hanukkah."—George W. Bush, Washington, D.C., December 10, 2001

Resources (all nonpartisan)

In addition to online voter registration ("Register, Pray, Vote"), Sojourners (sojonet.org) offers a weekly e-zine, called SojoMail with information and commentary "to help you practice spirituality and values at work, at home, in your community, and on the go." You can also buy a subscription to "Preaching the Word," which aims to connect social issues to the scriptures.

Some examples of nonpartisan groups' activities: United Church of Christ's (UCC.org) Web site has a set of resources including nonpartisan voter guides, information on issues and messages, a valuable guide to dos and don'ts about the church and politics, and voter registration information. NETWORK (networklobby.org) is a national Catholic Social Justice Lobby that, among other things, monitors congressional voting on key issues. The Religious Action Center of Reformed Judaism (rac.org) mobilizes the American Jewish Community on social issues and runs a resource-rich Web site. Council on American Islamic Relations (cair-net.org) focuses on voter registration and other issues. The Unitarian Universalist Association (uua.org) is asking Unitarians to register at least ten people. The American Friends Service Committee (www.afsc.org) is also promoting voter registration and other activities.

48. FIGHT FOR FAIR ELECTIONS

The Florida election fiasco in 2000 was as demoralizing as it was bizarre.

But a least Republicans and Democrats in Congress got the point that something was wrong with America's voting machines. They joined together and allocated billions of dollars to upgrade voting machines across the country. This is good. A flashback of the Florida debacle would be unbearable, especially if Katherine Harris were featured again.

But unfortunately this nightmare—or something even worse—is a real possibility.

The problem is that states are replacing their old voting machines with computerized ones that are vulnerable to the same problems as other computer technology, including crashes, power outages, viruses, and hacking.

Fortunately, this is an unusual case where there's a simple solution:

☞ Public election officials must be given full access to the touch-screen voting technology in order to limit fraud and unintentional errors.

☞ All voting machines should produce a voter-verifiable paper trail that could be used in case a recount is necessary or other problems arise. Such a trail might take the form of a receipt for each voter, which he or she could review prior to leaving the polls.

It's unlikely that Congress and President Bush will agree on a bill to mandate these remedies prior to the 2004 election, despite efforts by Representative Rush Holt (D-NJ) and others.

So, it's up to citizens to pressure another group of elected officials who can insist that computer voting machines produce a paper trail: secretaries of state, who are in charge of state elections.

Already, the secretaries of state of California and Nevada have decreed that touchscreen voting machines in their states must include a voter-verified paper trail. Other secretaries of state should be asked to do the same.

 for practical, concerned, and busy people.

Pick up the phone and call your secretary of state's office. Tell him or her that you want computer voting machines to produce a voter-verified paper trail.

 for anti-Bush patriots with time to spare.

Urge your friends to take action. E-mail your friends a summary of this chapter as well as the phone number for calling their secretary of state, wherever they live.

 for the anybody-but-Bush guerilla.

Personally deliver your letter to your secretary of state's office.

Bushism

"I'm hopeful. I know there is a lot of ambition in Washington, obviously. But I hope the ambitious realize that they are more likely to succeed with success as opposed to failure."
—George W. Bush, in an interview
with the Associated Press, January 2001

Resources

Learn more about this issue by visiting verifiedvoting.org or calvoter.org/votingtechnology.html.

TrueMajority.org has mobilized people nationally on this issue.

49. STAY INFORMED ABOUT LATE-BREAKING ACTIONS AND ISSUES

As the election gets closer and the dynamics and issues change, you'll need a few up-to-date sources of information on more ways you can show George the door in 2004.

The Internet has made tracking political campaigns and tapping into timely actions easy.

For action ideas, delivered fresh to your inbox, sign up with a few of the organizations we've listed in Chapter 5, Help Defeat Bush in Swing States (Even if You Don't Live in One), and Chapter 6, Educate People about an Issue You Care About.

Read through the lists in those chapters, select an organization, visit its Web site, or call and sign up for updates.

Progressive publications and their Web sites, like *In These Times*, *Mother Jones*, *The Nation*, *The Progressive*, *Utne Reader*, Z *Magazine*, are good sources of information.

Online news and information sources will provide you with perspectives on the issues and sometimes offer articles about things you can do.

Alternet.org is an online news service offering original and previously published material. Alternet will be providing ongoing election news, including a weekly political advice column, "Auntie Establishment," as well as updates on the most effective work of the anti-Bush campaign. Sign up on the Alternet.org Web site.

Bushrecall (bushrecall.org) distributes a daily e-mail update on Bush blunders and ways to stop him.

Bushwatch is a daily Internet magazine focused on you know who.

Buzz Flash (buzzflash.com) also provides a broad range of political news and opinion.

Center for Responsive Politics (opensecrets.org) is a nonpartisan research group that tracks money in politics. It provides excellent information on contributions to political campaigns.

In addition to providing news headlines and opinion from a progressive perspective, **Common Dreams** (commondreams.org) collects and distributes news releases from progressive nonprofit organizations.

Democrats.com, a Web site for progressive Democrats, distributes a good newsletter with facts and action ideas. On its Web site, click on "Community" on the left of the homepage and then on "Newsletters."

Fairness and Accuracy in Reporting (fair.org) is a nonpartisan media watchdog organization based in New York. It exposes neglect and bias in the news, including campaign news.

Freepress.org is a good source of opinion and political news.

Media Channel (MediaChannel.org) offers commentary and news from an international network of organizations and publications.

MichaelMoore.com mixes action ideas with devastating Bush critiques.

Stop Bush in 2004 (StopBushin2004.com) provides useful action-oriented information and resources.

TomPaine.com features news and opinions that are underplayed in the mainstream media. The organization is known for its advertisements spotlighting progressive issues on the *New York Times* op-ed page.

Truthout.org sends out a daily newsletter with useful action ideas and news.

for practical, concerned, and busy people.

Sign up for information from a handful of organizations or news sites on the Web. Send links for your favorite sites to e-mail contacts.

 for anti-Bush patriots with time to spare.

Sign up for information from at least ten organizations or news sites on the Web.

 for the anybody-but-Bush guerilla.

Read it all. Contrary to their reputation for being mindless knee-jerk reactionaries, true guerillas devour information of all types so they can think like their opponents—and understand their passive allies as well as they understand themselves.

Bushism

"I think we agree, the past is over."—George W. Bush, *Dallas Morning News*, May 10, 2000

Resources

See the list of online news and information sources on p. 167 and in Chapter 5, Help Defeat Bush in Swing States (Even if You Don't Live in One), and Chapter 6, Educate People About an Issue You Care About.

★ WE CAN WIN ★

50. HAVE FAITH

Especially with a guy like George W. Bush in the White House, it's not easy to believe that you can make a difference. The more evil he gets away with, the more insignificant you can feel and the more alienated. At least that's how we feel sometimes.

With Bush, Cheney, and company in your mind's backdrop, you might think that taking a small action—like putting a sticker on your car's bumper—will make you feel even more powerless. Ironically, though, taking any action—however insignificant in itself—will make you feel like you can help create a better world (well, most of the time), and take back our country.

Why? Because when you act, you understand that you are not alone—that there are millions and millions of people out there who share our values.

Getting started, in the shadow of the awesome apathy and chaos that surrounds us, is probably the most difficult part.

Maybe this quote from Robert Kennedy will help:

> *Each time a person stands up for an ideal, or acts to improve the lot of others, or strikes out against injustice, he or she sends a tiny ripple of hope. Crossing each other from a million different centers of energy and daring, these simple ripples build a current that can sweep down the mightiest walls of oppression and resistance.*

We understand that it's not necessarily reassuring to think of oneself as a tiny ripple in the sea of madness that has overtaken our country. A certain amount of faith is required to get going—faith that we can work together and win, faith that the right wing isn't smarter or better organized than we can be, and faith in each other.

Bushism

"One year ago today, the time for excuse-making has come to an end."—George W. Bush, Washington, D.C., January 8, 2003

Resources

Your own determination and realism.

Part 2

AN ELECTION PRIMER: SWING STATES, THE ELECTORAL COLLEGE, AND MORE

In the 2000 election, Gore won the popular vote (more people voted for him) but Bush won the actual presidency. Apart from the issues of irregular and questionable vote counting in certain Florida counties, which we won't get into here but about which volumes have already been written, Bush won the presidency because he received the majority of the votes of the Electoral College.

Huh?

Yeah, we all learned this in high school civics, but it was kinda like algebra: we never paid all that much attention because we never thought we'd need to use it. However, if we're going to unseat Bush in 2004, we need to use it.

Here's a primer:

The Electoral College

Under the Electoral College system, we do not elect the president and vice president through a *direct* nationwide vote. When you vote in a presidential election, you are actually voting for *electors* who later vote at a meeting of the Electoral College to select the president and vice president.

In 48 of the 50 States (and D.C.), the presidential ticket that wins the popular vote is awarded *all* the electoral votes for that state.[1] In other words, it's winner take all, because whichever candidate wins the popular vote in the state wins all the state's Electors. For example, all 55 of California's electoral votes go to the winner of that state's popular election, even if the margin of victory of the direct vote in California is only 500 votes. At the Electoral College, California's electors will all be voting for the same party ticket, no matter how close the popular vote is.

The candidate who wins the majority of electoral votes nationally wins the presidency. In December, after the November election, the electors from each state gather in their respective state capitals, and— barring unlikely exceptions—formally cast their votes for the ticket (president/vice president) that triumphed in their state.

This state-by-state, winner-takes-all rule is what worked in Bush's favor in 2000. (Were it not for that, our world would be a lot cleaner and more peaceful today.)

Each state is allotted a number of electoral votes equal to its number of Senators (two) plus its number of members in the United States House of Representatives (depends on state population). States with high populations thus have more electoral votes than less populated ones. The total number of electoral votes throughout the country is 538. To become president, a candidate must win a majority of the electoral votes, or at least 270. In 2000, Gore received 266 electoral votes, while Bush received 271 electoral votes.[2] (There was one abstention.)

Now, the Electoral College may be a constitutional relic, but it's our constitutional relic. And, we've gotta dance with the one who brung us, which is to say that we have to work within the Electoral College system to vote Bush out next time 'round.

---

[1] Only Nebraska and Maine do not follow the winner-takes-all rule.

[2] The National Archives and Record Administration. 2000 Electoral College Information. http://www.archives.gov/federal_register/electoral_college/votes_2000.html.

Swing States

Because state-by-state electoral votes decide the winner, presidential elections are really fifty-one separate contests for the electoral votes of each state (and D.C.). Presidential candidates, then, devise strategies and allocate resources across the states to produce a majority in the Electoral College. The national election essentially becomes a coordination of fifty-one individual elections.

Which brings us to the issue of "swing states."

Certain states, such as Texas, are virtually guaranteed to vote for Bush in 2004. Others, such as Massachusetts, are practically certain to go Democratic. The states that aren't a sure bet—and the definition of this varies, depending on whom you talk to—are known as the swing states.

Standard political strategy holds that candidates don't waste their time in states that are all sewn up, one way or the other. Kerry shouldn't bother in Texas or in Massachusetts, according to this theory. In Texas he doesn't have a prayer, and Massachusetts is already in his pocket.

Courting the swing states is a time-honored tradition in presidential politics. Campaigns are structured around the magic number, 270. Candidates spend more time and money in states whose high numbers of electoral votes could clinch a win, and sometimes ignore states whose small numbers of votes might be inconsequential in the final count.

However, sometimes a "small" state can make a huge difference, as New Hampshire did in 2000. Bush won New Hampshire by 7,211 votes, giving him four Electoral College votes. These four votes would have won the presidency for Gore. Incidentally, Green Party candidate Ralph Nader garnered 22,188 votes in New Hampshire. (Nader got less than 3 percent of the popular vote nationwide but did win enough votes in Florida and New Hampshire to tip those states toward George Bush.)

For the 2004 election, many people are returning to the results from the 2000 election and identifying the states with the smallest margin between the Democratic and Republican popular vote. Topping that list are Florida (obviously), Pennsylvania, and Ohio.[3] All told, seventeen states were decided by fewer than seven percentage points in 2000.

State	Winner of Popular Vote	Margin
Arizona	Bush	6 percent
Arkansas	Bush	6 percent
Florida	Bush	537 votes, a heartbreakingly small fraction of 1 percent
Iowa	Gore	1 percent
Maine	Gore	5 percent
Michigan	Gore	5 percent
Minnesota	Gore	2 percent
Missouri	Bush	3 percent
Nevada	Bush	4 percent
New Hampshire	Bush	1 percent
New Mexico	Gore	Less than 1 percent
Ohio	Bush	4 percent
Oregon	Gore	Less than 1 percent
Pennsylvania	Gore	5 percent
Washington	Gore	5 percent
West Virginia	Bush	6 percent
Wisconsin	Gore	Less than 1 percent

While the swing states, to the extent they can be positively identified, are important, as activists we should avoid focusing too much energy on swing-state strategy to the exclusion of the rest of the country. First, we don't even know for sure which states will "swing." Second, to win, the Democratic campaign needs to gain momentum and visibility across the country, which will affect swing voters everywhere.

[3] http://www.reachm.com/amstreet/archives/000124.html

Part 3

VOTER REGISTRATION (AND MAIL-IN BALLOT) RESOURCES AND DEADLINES

Election rules and procedures vary by state. In most states you can obtain voter registration forms and mail-in ballot request forms by phone or via the Internet.

Via the Internet

For mail-in ballots request forms, visit firstgov.com/Citizen/Topics/Voting.shtml and click the "Absentee ballots" button in the "Register to Vote and Go Vote" section. Check out regulations for your area.

For voter registration forms, try any of these nonpartisan Web sites: **League of Women Voters** (lwv.org/voter/register.html), **Rock the Vote** (rockthevote.org), **Sojourners** (sojo.net), and **Declare Yourself** (declareyourself.org). In most cases, you will be able to fill out the form online and print it out. Then sign it and mail it to the address provided.

By Phone

Call your secretary of state's office at the number listed below to request 1) a voter registration form or 2) a mail-in ballot request form. You can also ask about where you cast your ballot in person.

Secretary of State Phone Numbers

State	Secretary of State Contact
Alabama	334-242-7200
Alaska	907-465-4611
Arizona	602-542-4285
Arkansas	501-682-1010
California	916-653-6814
Colorado	303-894-2596
Connecticut	860-509-6000
Delaware	302-739-1111
District of Columbia	202-727-2525
Florida	850-245-6500
Georgia	404-656-2881
Hawaii	808-453-8683
Idaho	208-334-2300
Illinois	217-782-2201
Indiana	317-232-6531
Iowa	515-281-5204
Kansas	785-296-4564
Kentucky	502-564-3490
Louisiana	225-925-1000
Maine	207-626-8400
Maryland	410-974-5521
Massachusetts	617-727-7030
Michigan	517-322-1460
Minnesota	651-296-2803
Mississippi	601-359-1350
Missouri	573-751-4936
Montana	406-444-2304

Nebraska	402-471-2554
Nevada	775-684-5708
New Hampshire	603-271-3242
New Jersey	609-989-1900
New Mexico	505-827-3600
New York	518-474-4750
North Carolina	919-807-2000
North Dakota	701-328-2900
Ohio	614-466-2655
Oklahoma	405-521-3912
Oregon	503-986-1500
Pennsylvania	717-787-6458
Rhode Island	401-222-2357
South Carolina	803-734-2170
South Dakota	605-773-3537
Tennessee	512-463-5770
Texas	800-252-8683
Utah	801-538-1041
Vermont	802-828-2363
Virginia	804-371-0017
Washington	360-902-4151
West Virginia	304-558-6000
Wisconsin	608-266-8888
Wyoming	307-777-7378

Deadlines for Voter Registration and Mail-in Ballot Requests and Submission

If your questions are not answered by the table below, call your secretary of state's office at the number listed above. Or visit activoteamerica.com.

State	Voter Registration Deadline	Mail-in Ballot Deadlines
Alabama	10 days before an election. Applications must be postmarked or delivered by the eleventh day prior to the election.	Request an absentee ballot at any time up until 5 days before an election.
Alaska	30 days before the election.	Mail-in ballot applications must be received seven days before an election.
Arizona	29 days before the election.	Requests for an absentee ballot may be made up to 90 days prior to the election, but county election officials only start mailing absentee ballots 33 days prior to the election.
Arkansas	30 days before the election.	One-stop voting occurs on the Saturday 10 days before the election. Mailed-in ballots must be received no later than the day before the election.
California	15 days before the election.	Request an election ballot beginning 29 days and ending 7 days before the election.
Colorado	29 days before the election. If the application is received in the mail without a postmark, it must be received within 5 days of the close of registration.	Request an absentee ballot up to 2 days before the election.
Connecticut	14 days before the election.	Request an absentee ballot at any time before an election, except for the day of the election. County officials will mail ballots out 31 days before a general election and 21 days before a primary.

Delaware	20 days prior to the general election and 20 days prior to any primary election.	One-stop voting is available until noon the day before an election. Mailed-in ballots are due by the close of polls on Election Day. Requests for mail-in ballots must be received 4 days before the elec-
District of Columbia	30 days before the election.	Submit a request for an absentee ballot no later than 7 days before an election. Vote in person at the Board of Elections and Ethics beginning 14 days and ending 1 day before election day.
Florida	29 days before the election.	Call the Supervisor of Elections office to ask about an absentee ballot as soon as possible. Contact the election officials for more information.
Georgia	The fifth Monday before any general primary, general election, or presidential preference primary, or regularly scheduled special election pursuant to the Georgia Election Code. The fifth day after the date of the call for all other special primaries and elections.	Apply for an absentee ballot as early as 180 days before an election. The day before the election is the last day to apply for and receive an absentee ballot. Certain conditions on the application must be met.
Hawaii	30 days before the election.	Submit your application for an absentee ballot starting 60 days before the election. The last day to submit an application is 7 days before election day.
Idaho	25 days before the election, 24 day before for in person or register in person at the polls.	Request an absentee ballot by mail up until 6 days before the election. Vote absentee in person at the county clerk's office up until 5:00 p.m. the day before the election.

Illinois	29 days before the primary, 28 days before the general election.	Request an absentee ballot by mail beginning 40 days and ending 5 days before the election. Request and vote the absentee ballot in person starting 40 days before the election and no later than the day before the election.
Indiana	29 days before the election.	Request an absentee ballot starting 90 days before the election. Request an absentee ballot in person up until noon on the day before an election at the county elections office.
Iowa	Must be delivered by 5 p.m. 10 days before the election, if it is a state primary or general election; 11 days before all others. A postmark 15 or more days before an election is considered on time.	Request an absentee ballot by mail or in person 70 days before the election.
Kansas	Delivered 15 days before the election.	Request your absentee ballot at any time. County elections officials start sending out ballots 20 days before the election.
Kentucky	29 days before the election.	Absentee balloting is available upon application at least 7 days before date of election. Certain conditions on the application must be met.
Louisiana	30 days before the election.	Vote in person the week prior to the week of the election at the Registrar's office in your parish.

Maine	Delivered 10 business days before the election (or a voter may register in person up to and including election day).	Request an absentee ballot 90 days prior to the election. You may also vote absentee in person 30 to 45 days before the election at your municipal clerk's office.
Maryland	Postmarked 25 days before an election or received in the elections office by 9 p.m. no later than 21 days before an election.	Absentee balloting is allowed in Maryland under specific conditions.
Massachusetts	20 days before the election.	Apply for an absentee ballot for all elections in a year using one absentee ballot application. You may vote absentee in person at the county clerk's office 2 to 3 weeks before the election depending upon the type of the election.
Michigan	30 days before the election.	Absentee ballot requests must be in before 2:00 p.m. the Saturday before the election.
Minnesota	Delivered by 5:00 p.m. 21 days before the election (there is also Election Day registration at polling places).	Vote absentee in person on the Saturday and Monday before election day.
Mississippi	30 days before the election.	Request an absentee ballot 45 days before the election in person at the voter registrar's office. Absentee ballots can only be requested in person.
Missouri	28 days before the election.	Absentee ballot is available by application. (Online application is available.) In-person absentee voting begins 6 weeks prior to the election.

Montana	30 days before the election.	During the period beginning 75 days before the Election Day, and ending at noon the day before the election, you may apply to your Election Administrator for an absentee ballot.
Nebraska	The third Friday before the election (or delivered by 6 p.m. on the second Friday before the election).	Request an absentee ballot 120 days before the election. Vote absentee in person at you county elections office starting 35 days before and ending the day before the election.
Nevada	9:00 p.m. on the fifth Saturday before any primary or general election. 9:00 p.m. on the third Saturday before any recall or special election, unless held on the same day as a primary or general election. Then it remains on the fifth Saturday.	Vote absentee in person at the county clerk's office starting 12 days before and ending 4 days before the election.
New Hampshire	Voter registration forms must be received by city or town clerk by 10 days before the election. Register at polls on Election Day. (New Hampshire officials will only accept the National Voter Registration Form as a request for their own voter registration form.)	Absentee ballots are available from the town or city clerk 30 days prior to an election.
New Jersey	29 days before the election.	Mail-in absentee voter applications must be received by the county clerk at least 7 days prior to the election, or vote in person by 3:00 p.m. the day before election day.

New Mexico	28 days before the election.	Vote in person at your county clerk's office 20 days prior to the election.
New York	25 days before the election.	Request an absentee ballot beginning 30 days before and ending 7 days before the election day.
North Carolina	Postmarked 25 days before an election or received in the elections office or designated voter registration agency by 5 p.m.	Request a mail-in ballot beginning 50 days before and ending no later than the Tuesday prior to election day. Ballots are due by 5:00 p.m. the day before the election in order to be counted. Vote absentee in person up to 17 days before election day.
North Dakota	North Dakota does not have voter registration.	Request an absentee ballot any time before an election and the ballots will be made available to you starting 40 days prior to the election.
Ohio	30 days before the election.	Vote absentee if you will be absent on election day, are 62 or older, you or a family member are hospitalized, have a disability, are an elections official, are in jail, and for other reasons.
Oklahoma	25 days before the election.	Request an absentee ballot at anytime up until the Wednesday before the election.
Oregon	21 days before the election. (There is no deadline for applications for change of name, change of address, or to register with party.)	No absentee voting in Oregon since all ballots are mailed to registered voters.

Pennsylvania	30 days before an election or primary.	Absentee ballot application requirements vary in Pennsylvania depending upon the elector's category of eligibility. An absentee elector must file an application for an absentee ballot prior to each primary an election in which he or she is eligible to vote by absentee ballot.
Rhode Island	30 days before the election.	Absentee ballot requests must be received by the local board of canvassers no later than 21 days before the election.
South Carolina	30 days before the election.	If applying by mail, the county voter registration office must receive your application no later than 4 days prior to the election, or apply and vote in person up until 5:00 p.m. the day before an election.
South Dakota	15 days before the election.	Vote absentee in person up until the day of the election at the county auditor's office.
Tennessee	30 days before the election.	Vote absentee in person at the county election office starting 20 days before the election through the fifth day before the election. Absentee ballots must be requested from county elections office if voting by mail.
Texas	30 days before the election.	Once registered to vote, vote anytime starting 17 days before an election through the fourth day before election day. When requesting an absentee ballot by mail, request it 60 days before the election through the seventh day before the election.

Utah	20 days before an election.	For regular absentee voting, the county clerk should receive absentee ballot applications no later then the Friday before the election.
Vermont	Delivered to the town clerk before 12:00 noon, postmarked, or submitted to DMV on the second Sat. before an election.	Absentee ballot requests must be to the town clerk no later than 17 days before the election in order to receive a ballot.
Virginia	Delivered 29 days before the election.	Vote absentee in person at the office of the general registrar up until 3 days prior to the election.
Washington	30 days before the election or delivered in person up to 15 days before an election at a location designated by the county elections officer.	Request an absentee ballot up to 90 days before an election from the county auditor or election department.
West Virginia	20 days before the election.	Vote absentee in person 15 days before and ending 3 days before the election at the circuit clerk's office. If requesting a ballot automatically, either vote at the polls or request an absentee ballot for any given election.
Wisconsin	For municipalities where voter registration is required, 13 days before an election; or completed at the local voter registration office 1 day before an election; or completed at the polling place on election day.	Application must be received by the municipal clerk's office no later than 5:00 p.m. the Friday before the election day, or request in person no later than 5:00 p.m. the day before election day.

Wyoming	30 days before an election or register at the polling place on election day. However, Wyoming, by law, does not accept the National Voter Registration Form, which means you must use the state form.	Call or write the county clerk for details. Absentee ballots must be returned immediately to ensure they will be delivered to the county clerk's office not later than 7:00 p.m. on election day.

Sources of Nonpartisan Candidate Information:

Project Vote Smart (vote-smart.org)

Provides links for state-specific information. Has a wide range of facts for researching a candidate, from voting records to issue papers. Provides operators (1-800-VOTE-SMART) to give nonpartisan answers to your candidate and election questions over the phone!

The League of Women Voters (dnet.org)

Collects information from campaigns and sorts it by issue.

Part 4

FACTUAL AMMUNITION: A BITE-SIZED SUMMARY OF THE BUSH RECORD

With the election coming up on November 2, you need factual ammunition to fight Bush, organized for fast access and easy use. This is what we've provided below.

We've divided the facts about the atrocious record of the Bush administration into categories: job loss, growth of the federal deficit, tax policies, the environment, energy, education, AIDS, healthcare, women's right to choose, and Iraq.

For nonpartisan information on the candidates' positions on these and other issues, call Project Vote Smart's free voter research hotline (888-868-3762) or visit its Web site (vote-smart.org), or go to the League of Women Voters' Web site (dnet.org).

Job Loss

In the eight years before George W. Bush became president, the American economy added 21 million jobs.[1] **During President Bush's first three years in office, America has lost roughly 2.5 million jobs.**[2] That's the worst job loss record of any president since Hoover in the Great Depression.

In the three years since Bush took office, the unemployment rate has risen 40 percent—from 4 percent to 5.6 percent. Fewer than

---

[1] Bureau of Labor Statistics, "Employment, Hours, and Earnings from the Current Employment Statistics Survey (National)," Total Nonfarm Employment, 1993-2001 (data.bls.gov/cgi-bin/survey-most?ce).

[2] Bureau of Labor Statistics, "The Employment Situation: January 2004," February 6, 2004.

6 million Americans were unemployed at the beginning of Bush's term. By January 2004, 8.3 million Americans were looking for work.[3]

Growth of the Federal Deficit

In 2000, the year before Bush took office, the federal government posted a $127 billion surplus. In just three years, that surplus has been erased. It's estimated that **the federal deficit in 2003 was $401 billion—the largest deficit in American history**—and that it will reach close to $500 billion in 2004.[4]

Tax Policies

President Bush has pushed three major tax cuts, enacted in 2001, 2002, and 2003. Estimates for the total cost of these tax cuts range from $1.3 trillion to $1.9 trillion over eight to ten years.[5]

The Bush tax cuts provide little or no relief for working families—but they're a windfall for the wealthy.[6] Citizens for Tax Justice analyzed the three federal tax cuts President Bush has enacted and determined that:

☞ Each year from 2004 through 2010, taxpayers with annual incomes of less than $16,000 (the poorest 20 percent) will receive $100 or less in tax cuts.

☞ The wealthiest 1 percent of Americans—those with an annual income greater than $337,000—will receive, on average, $59,000 in 2004 and at least that much per year up to 2010, when they will receive $85,000.[7]

Members of the president's own party have begun to question Bush's economic policies. Republican Senator Olympia Snowe of Maine crit-

---

3 Bureau of Labor Statistics, "The Employment Situation: January 2004," February 6, 2004.

4 Congressional Budget Office, "The Budget and Economic Outlook: An Update," August 2003.

5 Tax Cut Compendium, TomPaine.com.

6 Fight For the Future: Election Information and Tools for SEIU Members (fightforthefuture.org/bushrecord/bush_jobs.cfm).

7 Citizens for Tax Justice, "The Bush Tax Cuts: The Most Recent CTJ Data, Average Tax Cuts Under the 2001-2003 Bush Tax Cuts by Calendar Year," July 2003.

icized Bush's 2004 tax cut, warning that it "may grow deficits to levels economists fear will be unsustainable."[8]

The Environment

Where do we begin on this one? The Bush presidency has been an utter catastrophe for the environment. And we're not the only ones who think so. Rep. Sherrod Brown (D-Ohio), a member of the Committee on Energy and Commerce, says, "There is an absolute hostility toward any positive strengthening of environmental law. It is a wholesale turning over to corporate America the governing of this country."[9]

The list of environmental disasters under Bush is so long that we had to subdivide it.

EPA decimation. In its first two years, the Bush administration cut 100 employees from the Environmental Protection Agency's (EPA) program that enforces our country's environmental laws.

Undermining of the Clean Air Act, the country's most important anti-pollution law, signed by Richard Nixon in 1970. In August 2003, the EPA announced it was adding a new "equipment replacement" exclusion to the New Source Review (NSR) rule of the Clean Air Act. The exclusion allows power plant operators and factories to keep the oldest, dirtiest plants online indefinitely without ever having to install the same modern pollution controls that newly built facilities are required to use.

Arsenic and old Bush. In April 2001, Bush rescinded Clinton's rule lowering permitted arsenic levels in drinking water from fifty to ten parts per billion. The administration later backed down, after studies and public outcry about the increased health risks. Too bad for the mining industry, which lobbied heavily to increase the limits.

Clear Skies Initiative. A complete misnomer. Compared to the Clean Air Act, this initiative will 1) allow twice as many sulfur dioxide emis-

---

8 MSNBC Local News, Seacoast Online, "N.H. GOP Lauds Bush Tax Cut," May 29, 2003.

9 *The I Hate Republicans Reader*, edited by Clint Willis, Thunder's Mouth Press, 2003.

sions, which cause acid rain and premature death from respiratory disease; 2) permit 50 percent more nitrous oxide emissions, which cause lung-damaging ozone smog, and 3) allow power plants to emit five times as much mercury.[10] In 2002, at least six million women of childbearing age in the United States had mercury levels in their bodies that exceeded those considered safe by the EPA.[11]

Gutting of environmental regulations. Since taking office, the Bush administration has gutted all of the following environmental rules, among others:[12]

☞ Regulations minimizing raw sewage discharges and requiring public notice of overflows.

☞ A rule prohibiting the federal government from awarding contracts to companies that violate federal laws, including environmental regulations.

☞ Forest service regulations giving watershed health, wildlife, and recreation higher priority than timber sales.

☞ Requirements that mining companies protect waterways and clean up mine-related pollution.

☞ A portion of the Endangered Species Act, requiring the Fish and Wildlife Service to respond to private lawsuits seeking to add new species to the list.

Energy

Campaign money. Energy companies were Bush/Cheney's biggest campaign contributors from the beginning. In 2000, oil and gas companies and their executives gave nearly $2 million to the Bush campaign. Bush's single biggest contributor from 1994 to 2000 was Enron. And it paid off. "Big time," as Dick Cheney would say.

---

10 "The Bush Administration's Air Pollution Plan," Natural Resources Defense Council Fact Sheet, February 2003.

11 Susan Schroeder, et.al., "Blood Mercury Levels in US Children and Women of Child-bearing Age," *Journal of the American Medical Association*, Volume 289, No. 13, April 2, 2003.

12 The Sierra Club, "Find the Remaining Safeguard" (sierraclub.org/bush/safeguard.asp).

The Anonymous Energy Task Force. Dick Cheney's Energy Task Force met behind closed doors in early 2001. The group was widely considered to be made up almost exclusively of energy industry executives, including Kenneth Lay, then chair of Enron. Cheney and his attorneys have so far fended off all attempts to unearth details about the group, which ultimately produced an energy policy highly favorable to oil and gas firms, the coal and nuclear industries, and other energy producers. A lower court has ruled that Cheney must turn over documents detailing who met with his task force, but in December 2003, the Supreme Court announced it would hear an appeal. Supreme Court Justice Antonin Scalia has refused to recuse himself from the trial, after legal ethics specialists questioned whether his going on a hunting trip with Cheney in January would affect his ability to be impartial in Cheney's case.

Climate Change. Bush reneged on his promise to require reductions in power plants' carbon dioxide emissions, which cause global warming. Bush also pulled out of the Kyoto Protocol, the international agreement to combat global warming, which 165 other nations signed in October 2001 and which called for modest reductions in greenhouse gas emissions. The decision came after frenetic lobbying by the coal mining and electric utility industries. At around the same time, the Bush administration deleted references to climate change from the Environmental Protection Agency's annual report on air pollution trends.

Education

Unfunded Education Mandates. Bush ran for office claiming he would be the "education president," and introduced a program he called "No Child Left Behind." He then submitted a 2003 budget that failed to cover the additional expenses imposed by his unfunded mandates requiring testing of students and teachers. The No Child Left Behind program was left more than $7 billion behind promised funding levels.[13]

---

[13] Rep. George Miller, House Education and the Workforce Committee, "Broken Promises: The GOP Record on Education," August 2003. See edworkforce.house.gov/democrats/brokenpromises.pdf.

Freeze on Pell Grants. While campaigning in 2000, Bush pledged to make college more affordable and accessible by increasing the maximum Pell Grant for college freshmen to $5,100. He has, of course, broken this promise. Just as college tuition is rising and the buying power of grants continues to erode, President Bush has frozen the maximum Pell Grant at $4,050 in his fiscal year 2005 education budget. This is the third year in a row that Bush has frozen or cut the maximum Pell Grant.[14]

Dismantling Head Start. The nonpartisan National Head Start Association warns that Bush's 2004 budget would begin a five-year process in which the highly successful federal program would be replaced with, "a hodgepodge of inconsistent and untested state government programs ... (that would) serve fewer children than Head Start does now or provide less comprehensive services to those children who are served."[15] The House Head Start bill modeled on Bush's proposal mandates a number of improvements in Head Start standards, but provides no funds to pay for those improvements.[16]

In May 2003, Bush's Department of Health and Human Services issued a letter threatening to discipline Head Start teachers and volunteers who criticized Bush's plan. The National Head Start Association called the letter "a callous attempt to terrify Head Start staff and volunteers into silence with the prospect of possible jail time."[17]

AIDS

Bush promised a comprehensive plan that would prevent seven million new AIDS infections, treat two million people with life-extending drugs—and provide humane care for millions of people suffering from AIDS, and for children orphaned by AIDS.[18] However, Bush then

[14] President Bush's FY 2004 Budget, Department of Education, A Preliminary Analysis; *New York Times*, March 10, 2003.

[15] National Head Start Association, "Dismantling Head Start," April 16, 2003.

[16] Center for Law and Social Policy, "Headed in the Wrong Direction: Why the House Head Start Bill (H.R. 2210) is Unlikely to Make the Program Better," July 11, 2003.

[17] *American Prospect* (Web edition), "Head Hunter: The Bush Administration Wants to Slash Head Start," July 10, 2003.

[18] George W. Bush, State of the Union Address, January 28, 2003.

under-funded his own proposal to fight AIDS by nearly $1 billion.[19]

Healthcare

Over three million more Americans lack health insurance now than when Bush entered office, bringing the total number of uninsured to 43.6 million.[20]

The cost of insurance is rising faster than workers' pay.[21] Benefit costs were up 1.2 percent in the fourth quarter of 2003, while wages were up less than half that.[22]

Bush's Medicare bill, signed into law in December 2003, is a disaster for those who need healthcare the most. President Bush's Medicare drug plan does not rein in the prices charged by drug companies; in fact, it *forbids* Medicare officials from negotiating for lower drug prices for seniors. Under the new Medicare drug plan, most Medicare beneficiaries will pay more out-of-pocket for prescription drugs in 2007 than they do today.[23] The bill gives the pharmaceutical industry $139 billion in profit.[24]

Women's Right to Choose

President Bush's anti-choice positions are well known, and he would likely have the opportunity—if elected to a second term—to appoint another anti-choice Supreme Court justice. In light of the Court's sharp divisions about abortion rights, it is probable that one more anti-choice justice would tip the scales against a women's right to choose, leaving it to individual states to determine whether abortion

[19] "The Senate's Last Chance on AIDS," *New York Times*, October 28, 2003.

[20] Robin Toner and Robert Pear, "State of the Union: Domestic Agenda," *New York Times*, Jan. 21, 2004.

[21] "Employee Contributions for Medical Insurance in 2003," Bureau of Labor Statistics, September 25, 2003; "Health Care Costs Increase Bargaining Pressures," Labor Research Association, April 30, 2003.

[22] CNN, *Lou Dobbs Tonight*, January 29, 2004, cnn.com/transcripts/040129/ldt.00.html.

[23] "Medicare Prescription Drugs: Too High a Price for Modest Benefit," Gail Shearer, Director of Health Policy Analysis, Consumers Union, November 17, 2003.

[24] "61 Percent of Medicare's New Prescription Drug Subsidy Is Windfall Profit to Drug Makers," Alan Sager and Deborah Socolar, Health Reform Program at Boston University's School of Public Health, October 31, 2003.

would remain legal, and this would cut off access to safe and legal abortions for women, particularly poor women, across America.

What's less known is the power that President Bush's right-wing supporters, who oppose all family planning, wield over this administration. For example, Bush has twice cut U.S. funding for the United Nations Population Fund (UNFPA), which is the world's leading multilateral source of funding for maternal-health programs and family-planning services operating in over 140 impoverished countries. The UNFPA receives contributions from over 120 nations, including Afghanistan, which gave $100 as a symbolic gesture to highlight just how critical the UNFPA is to poor countries.[25] Under pressure from right wing extremists opposed to family planning, Bush withheld America's annual contribution of $34 million for two consecutive years, based on the accusation that the UNFPA supports forced abortions in China—a charge that no other nation in the world believes and that has been rejected by three U.S. fact-finding missions, including one conducted by President Bush's own State Department. (Even the U.S. Congress apparently doesn't believe the accusation, because it twice passed the UNFPA money, only to have Bush withhold it from the UNFPA.) The victims in Bush's extremist political game are real people: UNFPA experts estimate that the $34 million cut by Bush could lead each year to two million unwanted pregnancies, 800,000 induced abortions, 4,700 maternal deaths, and 77,000 infant and child deaths.[26]

Iraq

The push for war by the Bush administration, the empty justifications for the war, Bush's ignoring the majority of the world's opinion that the United States should not unilaterally invade Iraq, the colossal intelligence failure that led Congress to authorize the war in Iraq, and Bush's refusal to accept responsibility for acting on faulty intelligence are all deeply disturbing.

[25] United Nations Population Fund (unfpa.org).
[26] 34 Million Friends of the UNFPA, "News Releases," March 1, 2004 (34millionfriends.org); Molly Ivins, "Another Slap against Women," *Chicago Tribune*, October 22, 2002.

"We Were All Wrong." In January 2004, David Kay, the Bush appointee who led the American effort to find banned weapons in Iraq, testified before Congress that Iraq had no stockpiles of chemical and biological weapons at the start of the war.[27] After stepping down from his post, Kay said "we were almost all wrong" about weapons of mass destruction in Iraq and that his search there found no evidence of biological or chemical arms.[28]

The Administration's Scramble. After Kay's statement, members of the Bush administration scrambled to defend their respective positions. Secretary of Defense Donald Rumsfeld told Congress that it was "possible, but not likely" that Iraq had not had weapons of mass destruction at the start of the war.[29] Vice President Dick Cheney said, in an interview on National Public Radio, that it would "take some additional, considerable period of time in order to look in all the cubby holes and the ammo dumps and all the places in Iraq where you might expect to find something like that."[30] Mr. Kay's testimony is widely believed to refute both Cheney's and Rumsfeld's remarks.

The Intelligence Response. In response to Kay's remarks about the colossal intelligence failure, George Tenet, the director of the CIA, said that CIA analysts had never said that Iraq posed an imminent threat, but that they had judged that Iraq was several years away from making a nuclear weapon and had always spelled out their areas of disagreement. According to a *New York Times* editorial, "Those sounded like warning shots against scapegoating the intelligence community for exaggerations made by higher-ups who were pushing for war."[31]

---

[27] Richard W. Stevenson, "Iraq Illicit Arms Gone Before War, Inspector States," *New York Times*, January 23, 2004.

[28] "Kay Says Everyone Wrong on WMD," ABC News Online, January 29, 2004.

[29] "The Administration's Scramble," *New York Times*, February 6, 2004.

[30] "Cheney: U.S. to Continue Search for Weapons of Mass Destruction," National Public Radio, January 22, 2004.

[31] "The Administration's Scramble," *New York Times*, February 6, 2004.

Pushing for War. Paul O'Neill, the Bush-appointed Secretary of Treasury who resigned in December 2002, has stated that from Bush's first cabinet meeting—long before September 11—getting rid of Saddam was central to the Bush agenda. O'Neill is quoted as saying, "From the start, we were building the case against Hussein and looking at how we could take him out and change Iraq into a new country....And, if we did that, it would solve everything.... That was the tone of it—the president was saying, 'Fine. Go find me a way to do this.'"[32]

The Buck Stops Somewhere Else. On *Meet the Press* on February 8, 2004, Tim Russert posed this question to President Bush: "But can you launch a pre-emptive war without iron-clad, absolute intelligence that he had weapons of mass destruction?" Throughout the interview, President Bush continually refused to accept responsibility for leading the United States into war based on flawed intelligence. If the president does not hold himself accountable for every aspect of undertaking a war and endangering the lives of U.S. soldiers, who is responsible?

[32] Ron Suskind, *The Price of Loyalty: George W. Bush, the White House, and the Education of Paul O'Neill*, Simon & Schuster, 2004.